UPERHEROES ON A MEDICAL MISSION

...ITH PAULINA?"
...OOD ALLERGIES

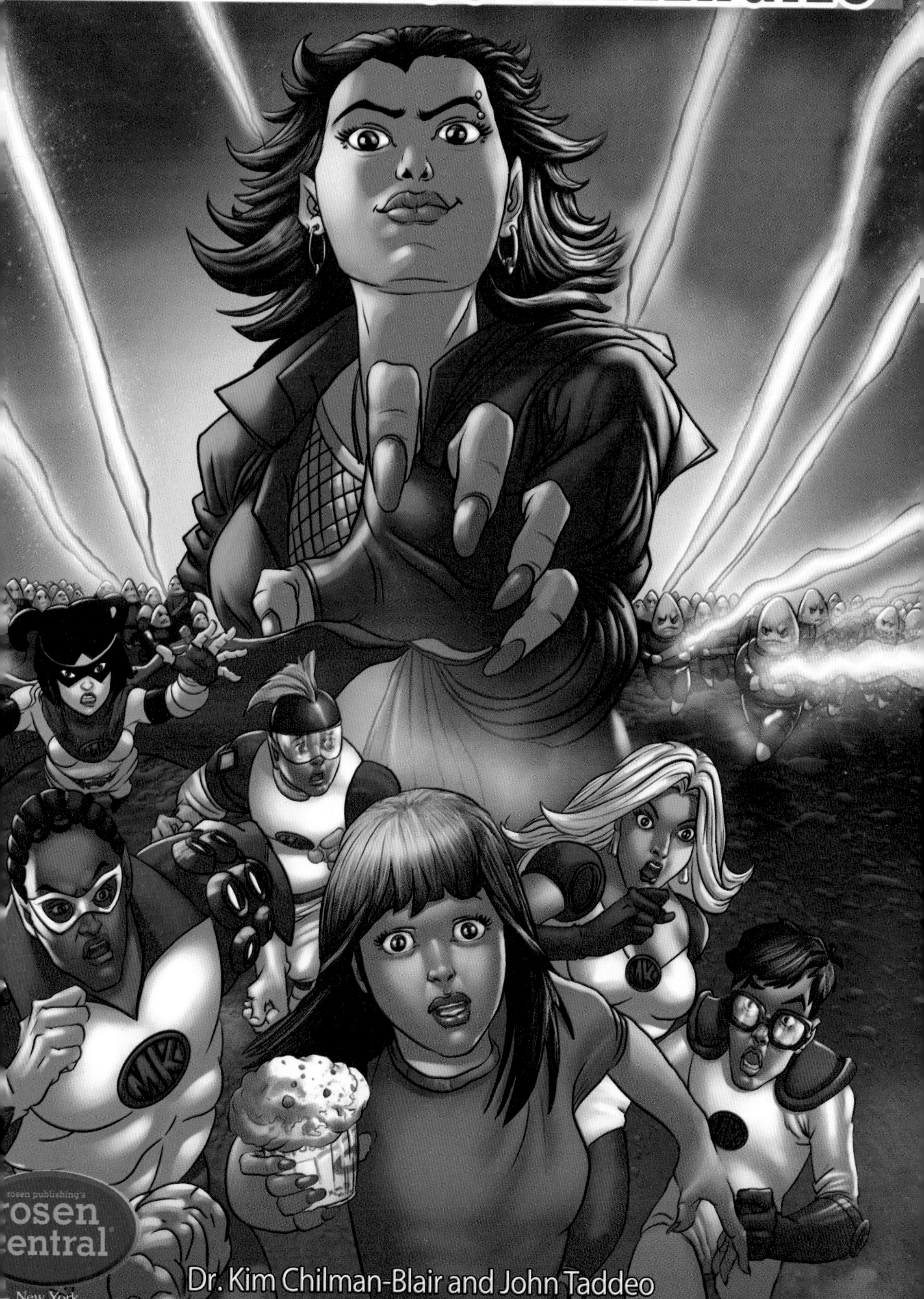

rosen publishing's
rosen central
New York

Dr. Kim Chilman-Blair and John Taddeo
Medical content reviewed for accuracy by Professor John Warner

This edition published in 2010 by:

The Rosen Publishing Group, Inc.
29 East 21st Street
New York, NY 10010

Library of Congress Cataloging-in-Publication Data

Chilman-Blair, Kim.
"What's up with Paulina?": medikidz explain food allergies / Dr. Kim Chilman-Blair and John Taddeo; medical content reviewed for accuracy by Professor John Warner.
        p. cm.—(Superheroes on a medical mission)
Includes index.
ISBN 978-1-4358-3537-5 (library binding)
1. Food allergy in children—Comic books, strips, etc. I. Taddeo, John. II. Title.
RJ386.5.C45 2010
618.92'975—dc22

                                                                                    2009031614

Manufactured in China

CPSIA Compliance Information: Batch #MW0102YA: For Further Information contact Rosen Publishing, New York, New York at 1-800-237-9932

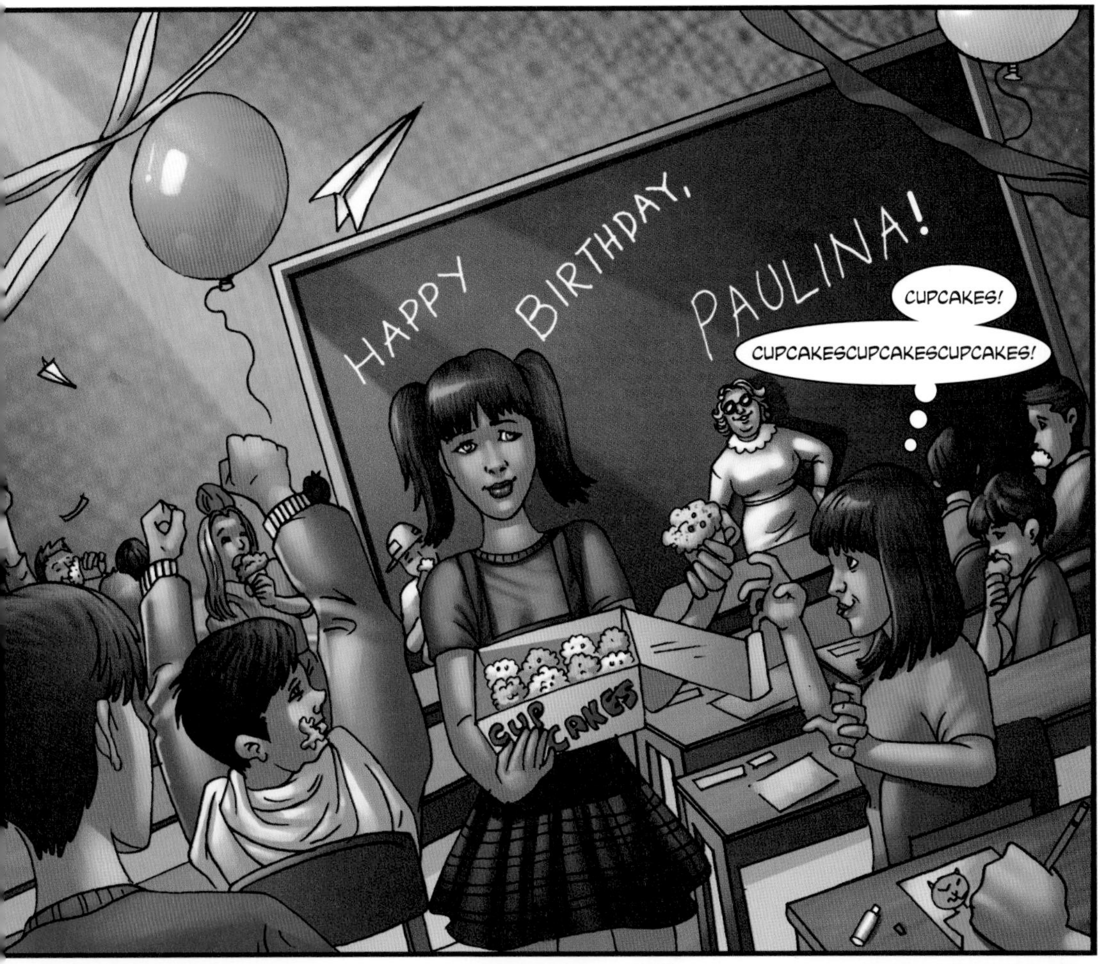
HAPPY BIRTHDAY, PAULINA!
CUPCAKES!
CUPCAKESCUPCAKESCUPCAKES!
CUP CAKES

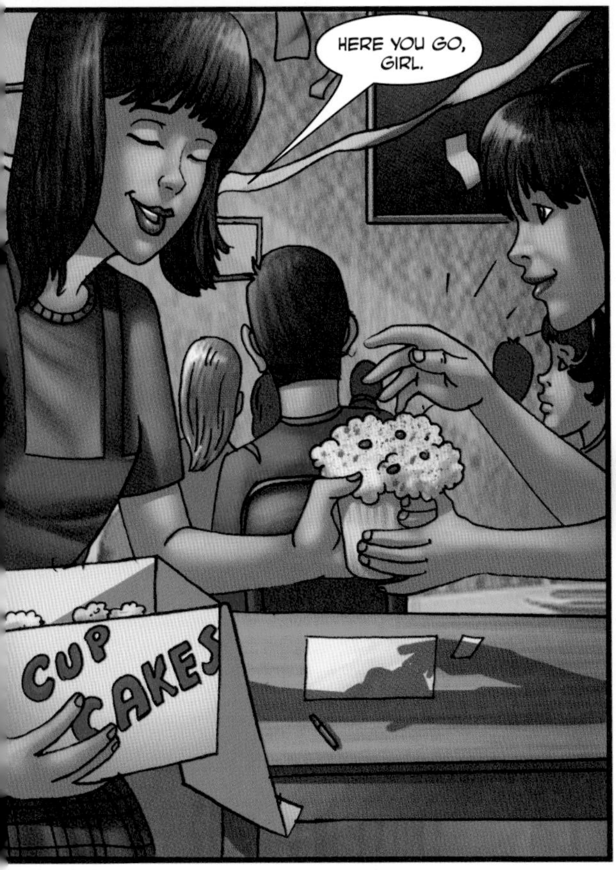
HERE YOU GO, GIRL.
CUP CAKES

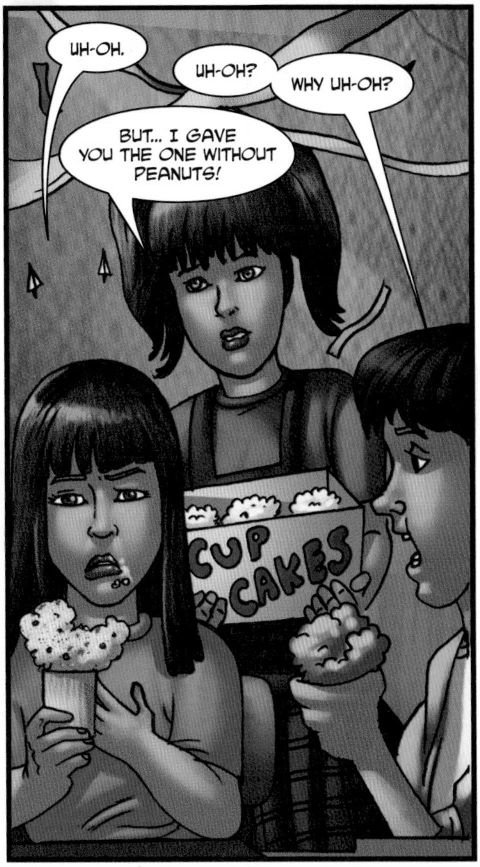
UH-OH.
UH-OH?
WHY UH-OH?
BUT... I GAVE YOU THE ONE WITHOUT PEANUTS!
CUP CAKES

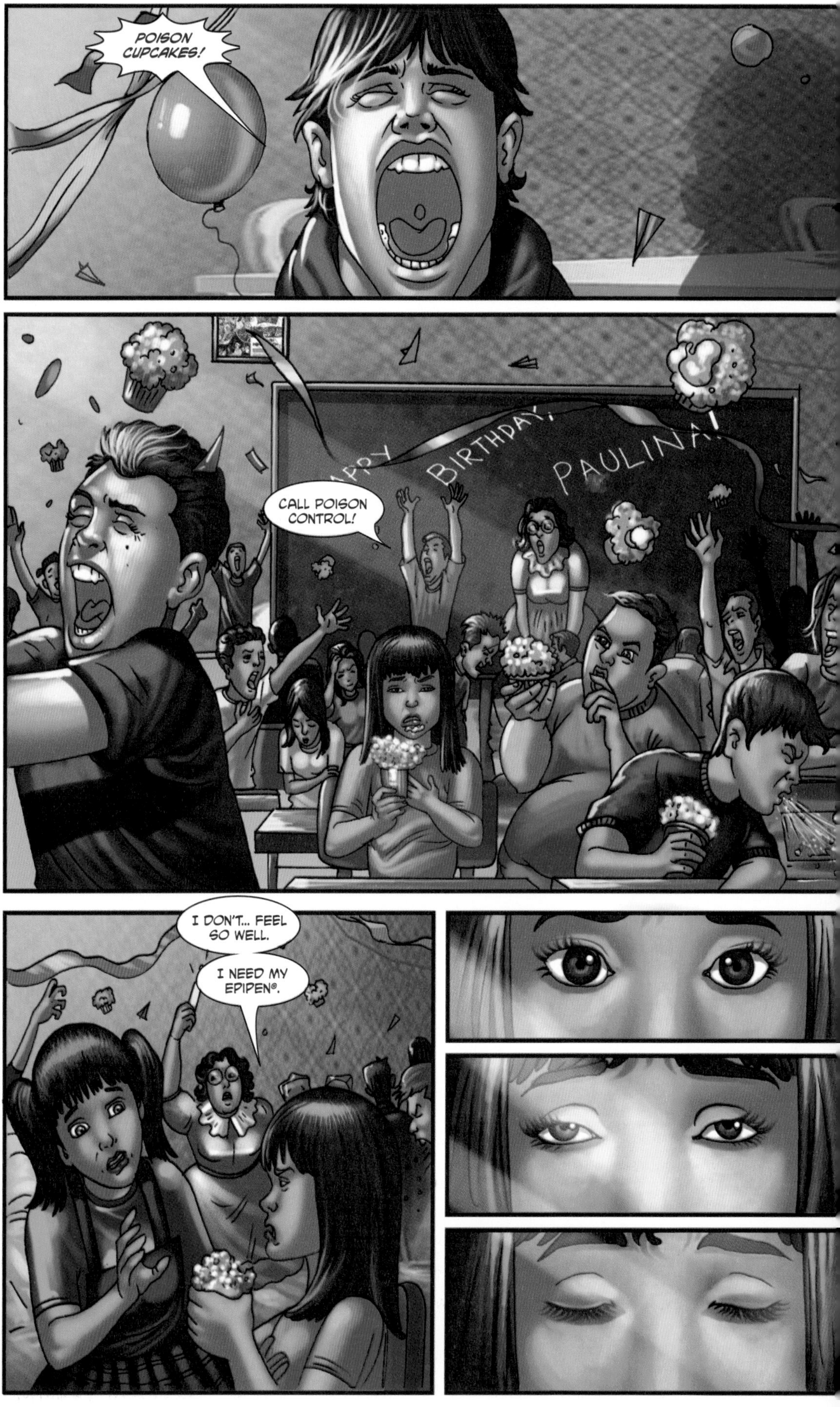
POISON CUPCAKES!
HAPPY BIRTHDAY PAULINA!
CALL POISON CONTROL!
I DON'T... FEEL SO WELL.
I NEED MY EPIPEN®.

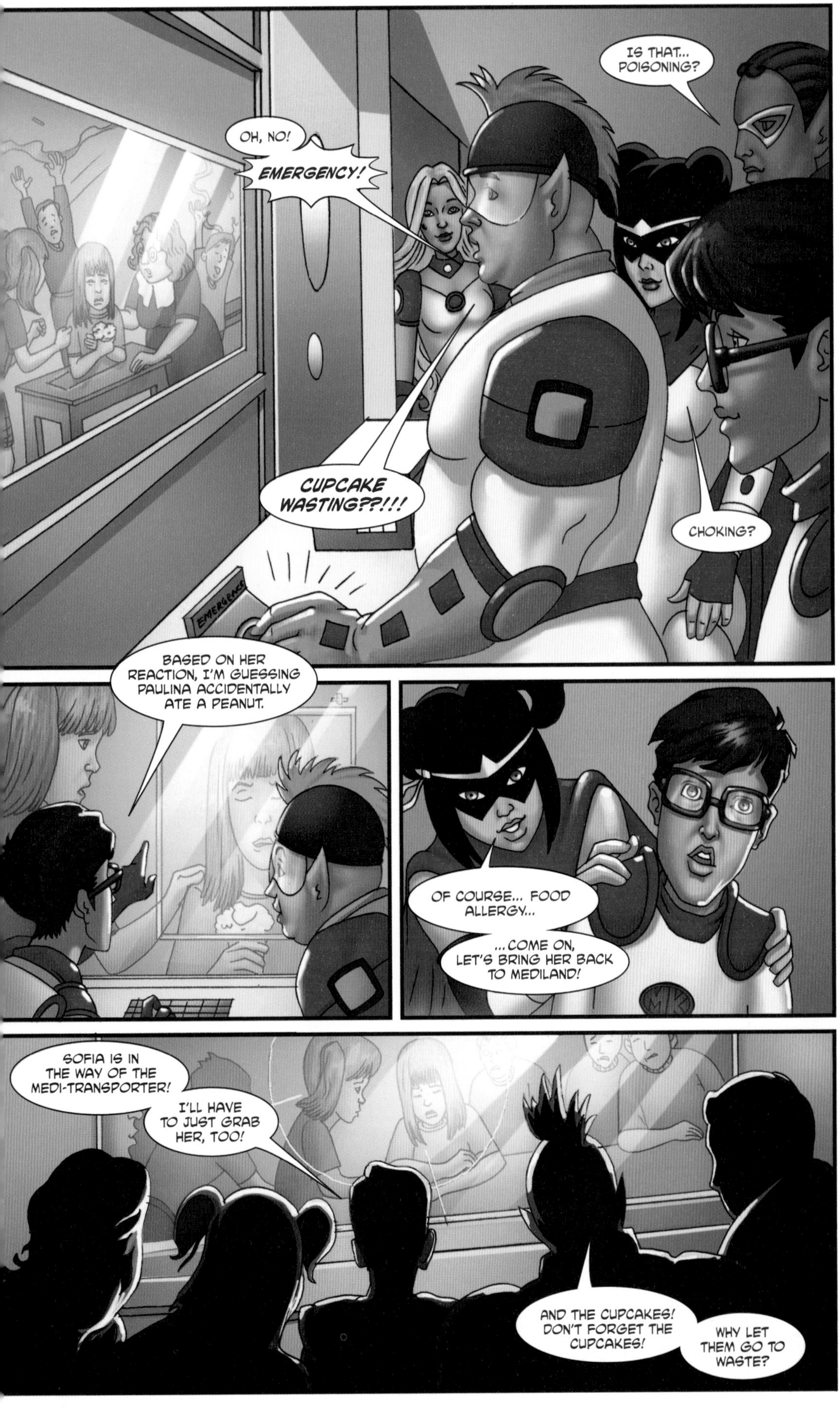
IS THAT... POISONING?
OH, NO!
EMERGENCY!
CUPCAKE WASTING??!!!
CHOKING?
BASED ON HER REACTION, I'M GUESSING PAULINA ACCIDENTALLY ATE A PEANUT.
OF COURSE... FOOD ALLERGY...
...COME ON, LET'S BRING HER BACK TO MEDILAND!
SOFIA IS IN THE WAY OF THE MEDI-TRANSPORTER!
I'LL HAVE TO JUST GRAB HER, TOO!
AND THE CUPCAKES! DON'T FORGET THE CUPCAKES!
WHY LET THEM GO TO WASTE?

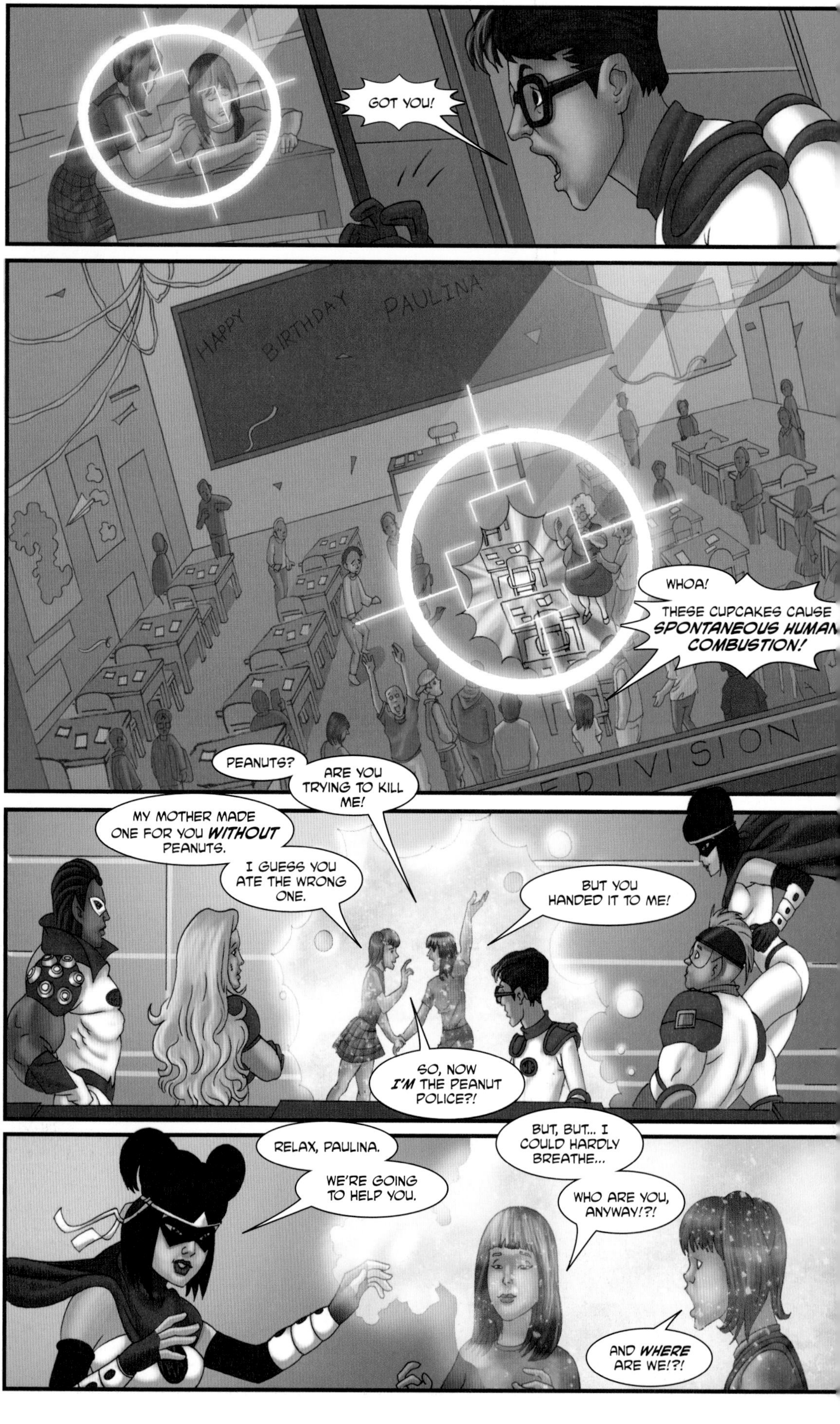
GOT YOU!
HAPPY BIRTHDAY PAULINA
WHOA!
THESE CUPCAKES CAUSE SPONTANEOUS HUMAN COMBUSTION!
DIVISION
PEANUTS?
ARE YOU TRYING TO KILL ME!
MY MOTHER MADE ONE FOR YOU WITHOUT PEANUTS.
I GUESS YOU ATE THE WRONG ONE.
BUT YOU HANDED IT TO ME!
SO, NOW I'M THE PEANUT POLICE?!
RELAX, PAULINA.
WE'RE GOING TO HELP YOU.
BUT, BUT... I COULD HARDLY BREATHE...
WHO ARE YOU, ANYWAY!?!
AND WHERE ARE WE!?!

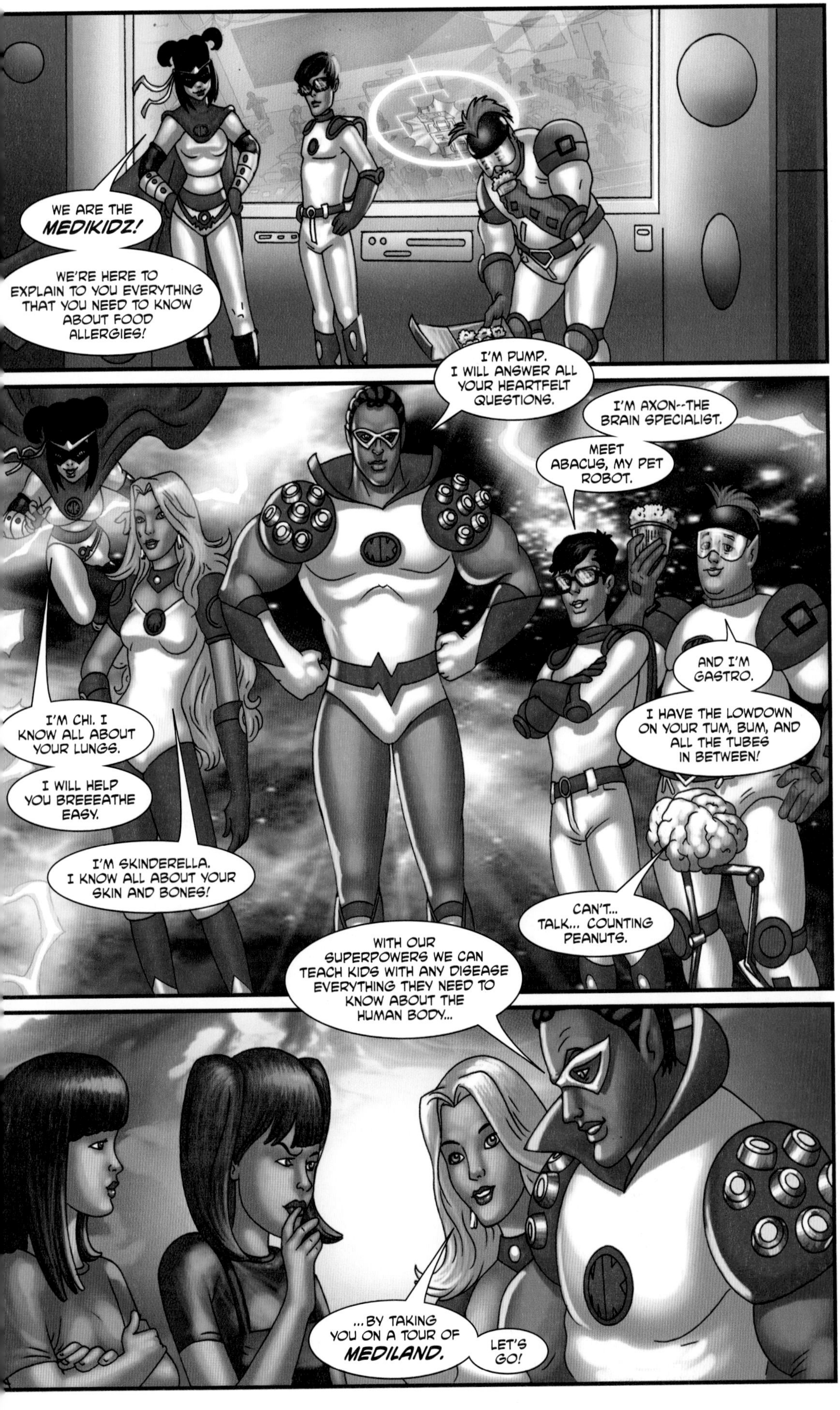
WE ARE THE MEDIKIDZ!
WE'RE HERE TO EXPLAIN TO YOU EVERYTHING THAT YOU NEED TO KNOW ABOUT FOOD ALLERGIES!
I'M PUMP. I WILL ANSWER ALL YOUR HEARTFELT QUESTIONS.
I'M AXON--THE BRAIN SPECIALIST.
MEET ABACUS, MY PET ROBOT.
AND I'M GASTRO.
I HAVE THE LOWDOWN ON YOUR TUM, BUM, AND ALL THE TUBES IN BETWEEN!
I'M CHI. I KNOW ALL ABOUT YOUR LUNGS.
I WILL HELP YOU BREEEATHE EASY.
I'M SKINDERELLA. I KNOW ALL ABOUT YOUR SKIN AND BONES!
CAN'T... TALK... COUNTING PEANUTS.
WITH OUR SUPERPOWERS WE CAN TEACH KIDS WITH ANY DISEASE EVERYTHING THEY NEED TO KNOW ABOUT THE HUMAN BODY...
...BY TAKING YOU ON A TOUR OF MEDILAND.
LET'S GO!

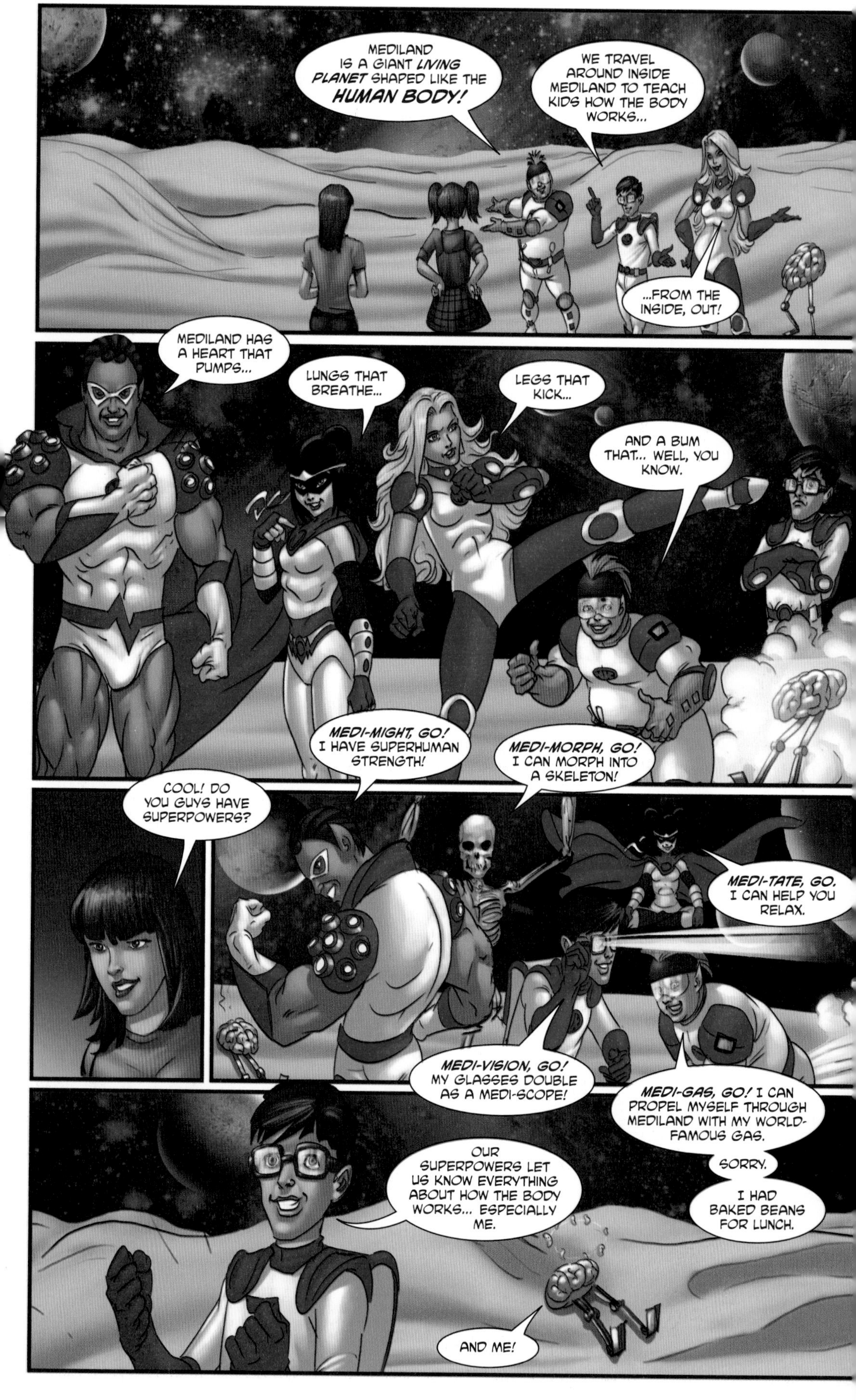
MEDILAND IS A GIANT *LIVING PLANET* SHAPED LIKE THE **HUMAN BODY!**
WE TRAVEL AROUND INSIDE MEDILAND TO TEACH KIDS HOW THE BODY WORKS...
...FROM THE INSIDE, OUT!
MEDILAND HAS A HEART THAT PUMPS...
LUNGS THAT BREATHE...
LEGS THAT KICK...
AND A BUM THAT... WELL, YOU KNOW.
COOL! DO YOU GUYS HAVE SUPERPOWERS?
MEDI-MIGHT, GO! I HAVE SUPERHUMAN STRENGTH!
MEDI-MORPH, GO! I CAN MORPH INTO A SKELETON!
MEDI-TATE, GO. I CAN HELP YOU RELAX.
MEDI-VISION, GO! MY GLASSES DOUBLE AS A MEDI-SCOPE!
MEDI-GAS, GO! I CAN PROPEL MYSELF THROUGH MEDILAND WITH MY WORLD-FAMOUS GAS.
SORRY.
I HAD BAKED BEANS FOR LUNCH.
OUR SUPERPOWERS LET US KNOW EVERYTHING ABOUT HOW THE BODY WORKS... ESPECIALLY ME.
AND ME!

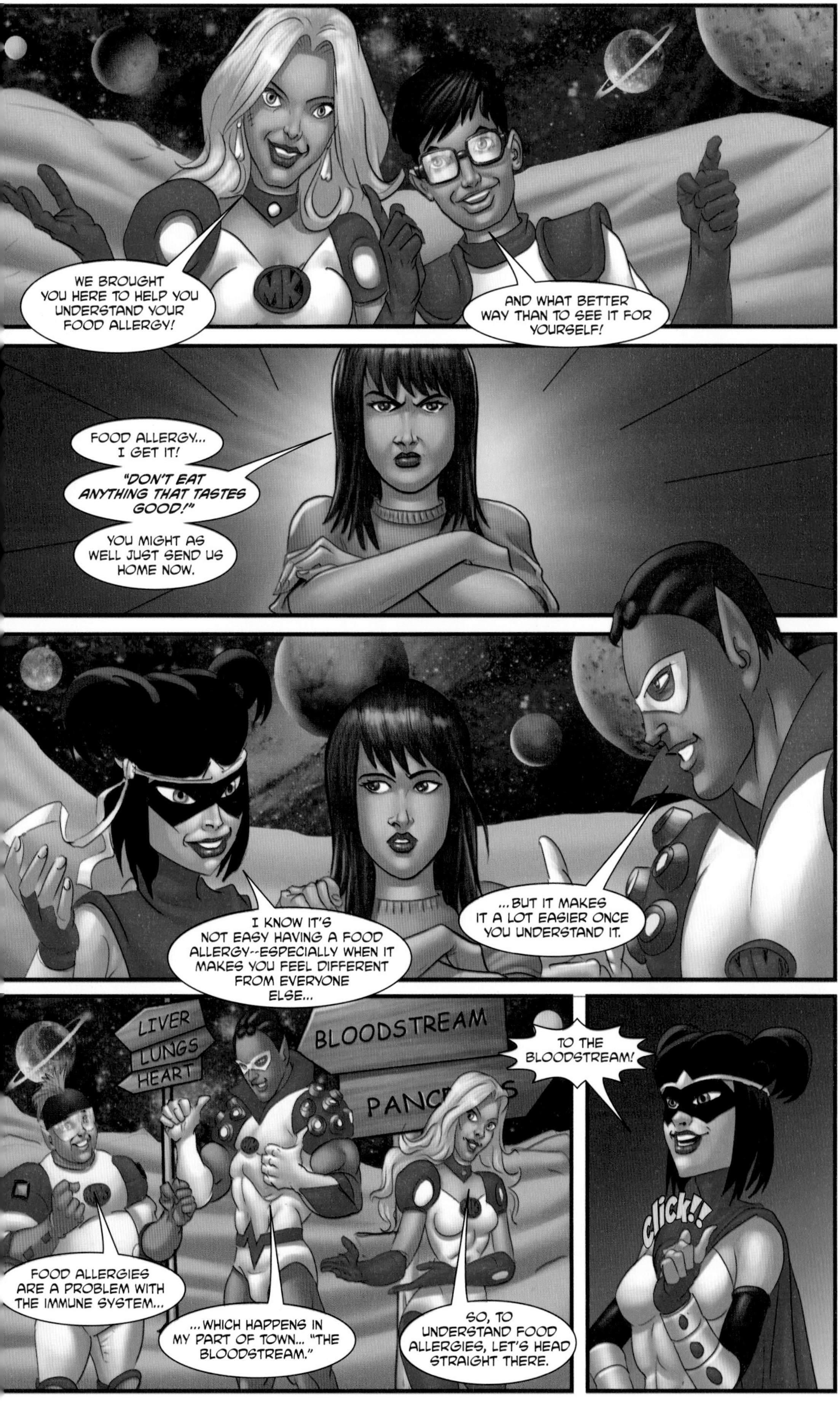
WE BROUGHT YOU HERE TO HELP YOU UNDERSTAND YOUR FOOD ALLERGY!
AND WHAT BETTER WAY THAN TO SEE IT FOR YOURSELF!
FOOD ALLERGY... I GET IT!
"DON'T EAT ANYTHING THAT TASTES GOOD!"
YOU MIGHT AS WELL JUST SEND US HOME NOW.
I KNOW IT'S NOT EASY HAVING A FOOD ALLERGY--ESPECIALLY WHEN IT MAKES YOU FEEL DIFFERENT FROM EVERYONE ELSE...
...BUT IT MAKES IT A LOT EASIER ONCE YOU UNDERSTAND IT.
LIVER
LUNGS
HEART
BLOODSTREAM
FOOD ALLERGIES ARE A PROBLEM WITH THE IMMUNE SYSTEM...
...WHICH HAPPENS IN MY PART OF TOWN... "THE BLOODSTREAM."
SO, TO UNDERSTAND FOOD ALLERGIES, LET'S HEAD STRAIGHT THERE.
TO THE BLOODSTREAM!
click!!

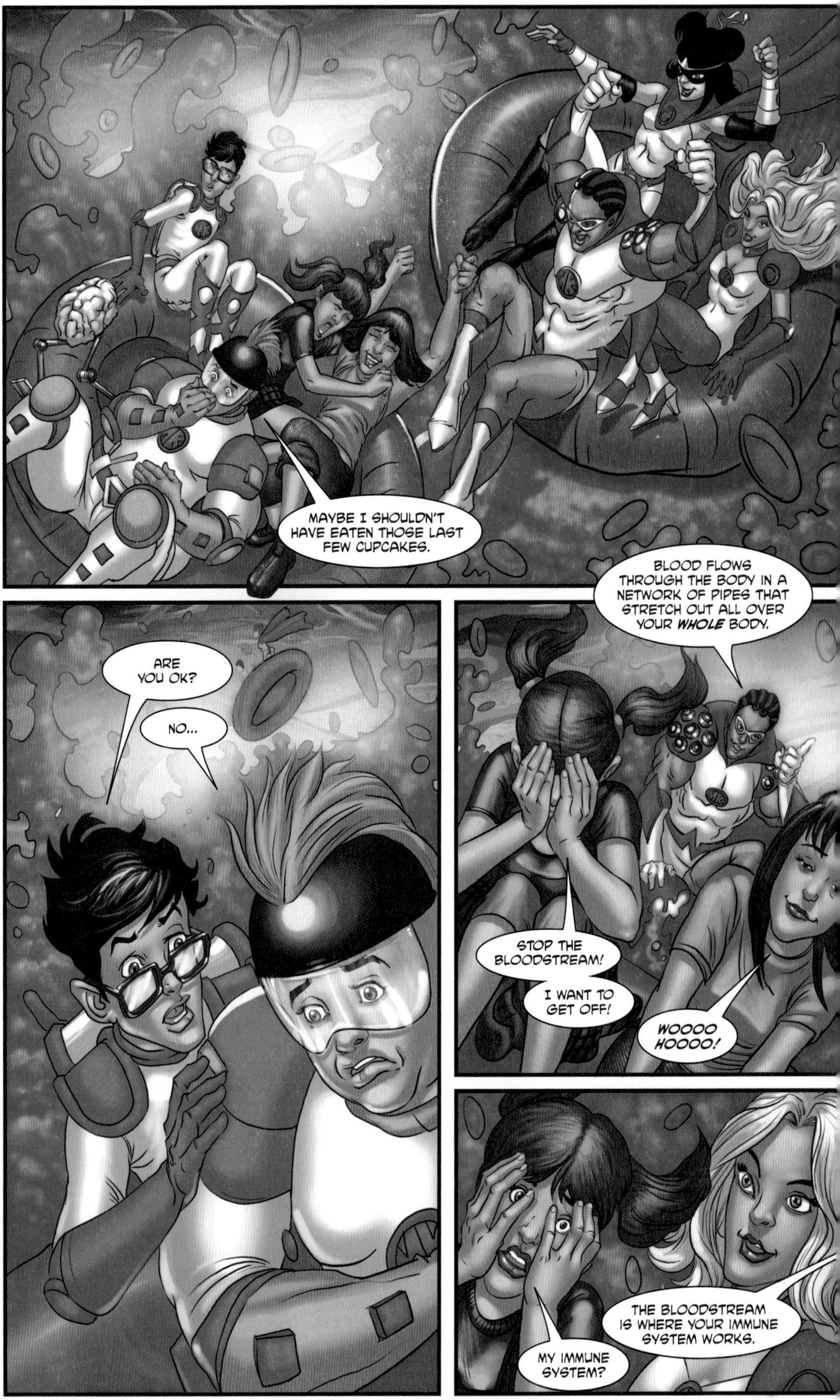
MAYBE I SHOULDN'T HAVE EATEN THOSE LAST FEW CUPCAKES.
BLOOD FLOWS THROUGH THE BODY IN A NETWORK OF PIPES THAT STRETCH OUT ALL OVER YOUR WHOLE BODY.
ARE YOU OK?
NO...
STOP THE BLOODSTREAM!
I WANT TO GET OFF!
WOOOO HOOOO!
THE BLOODSTREAM IS WHERE YOUR IMMUNE SYSTEM WORKS.
MY IMMUNE SYSTEM?

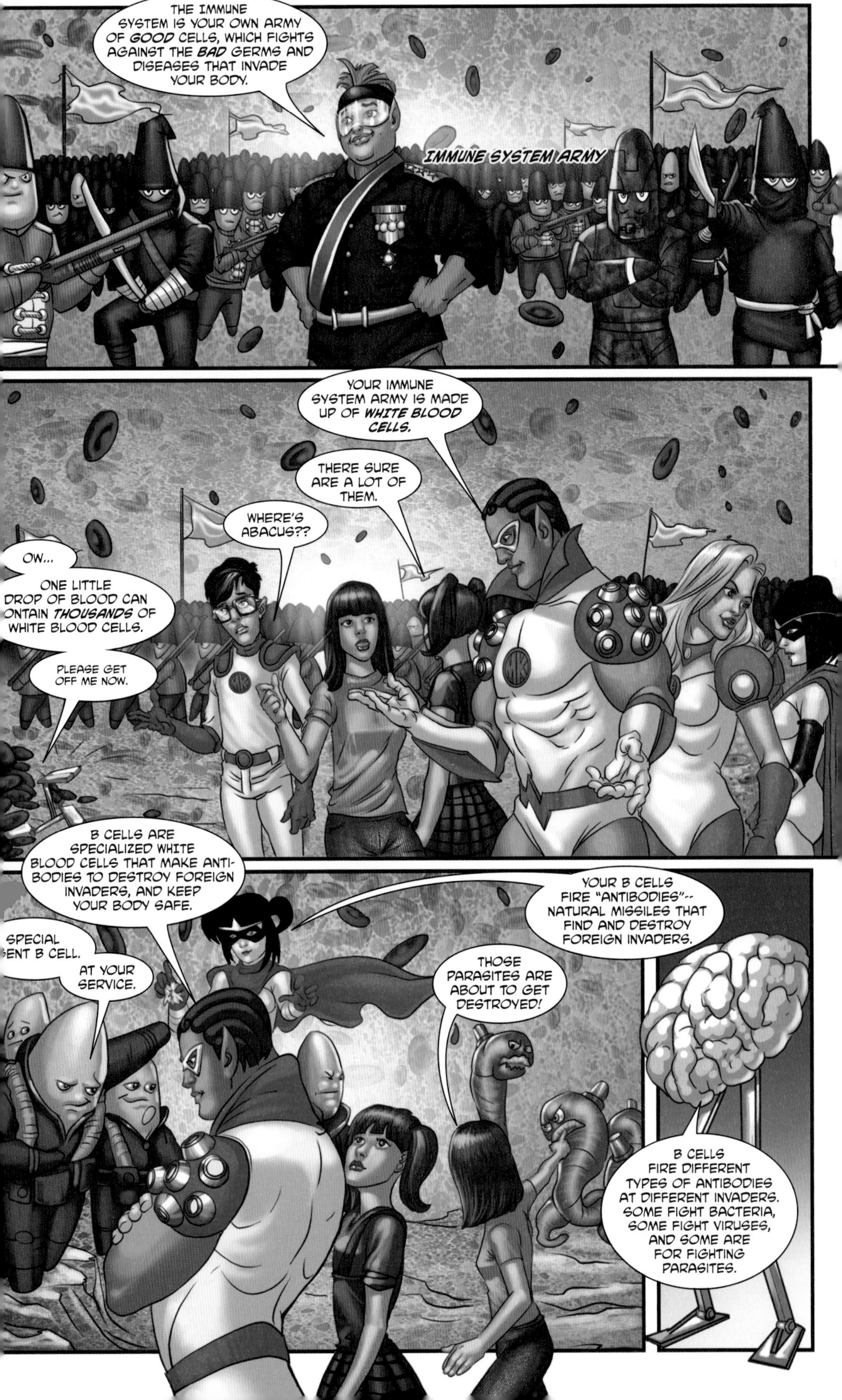
THE IMMUNE SYSTEM IS YOUR OWN ARMY OF *GOOD* CELLS, WHICH FIGHTS AGAINST THE *BAD* GERMS AND DISEASES THAT INVADE YOUR BODY.
IMMUNE SYSTEM ARMY
YOUR IMMUNE SYSTEM ARMY IS MADE UP OF *WHITE BLOOD CELLS.*
THERE SURE ARE A LOT OF THEM.
WHERE'S ABACUS??
OW...
ONE LITTLE DROP OF BLOOD CAN ONTAIN *THOUSANDS* OF WHITE BLOOD CELLS.
PLEASE GET OFF ME NOW.
B CELLS ARE SPECIALIZED WHITE BLOOD CELLS THAT MAKE ANTI-BODIES TO DESTROY FOREIGN INVADERS, AND KEEP YOUR BODY SAFE.
YOUR B CELLS FIRE "ANTIBODIES"-- NATURAL MISSILES THAT FIND AND DESTROY FOREIGN INVADERS.
SPECIAL ENT B CELL.
AT YOUR SERVICE.
THOSE PARASITES ARE ABOUT TO GET DESTROYED!
B CELLS FIRE DIFFERENT TYPES OF ANTIBODIES AT DIFFERENT INVADERS. SOME FIGHT BACTERIA, SOME FIGHT VIRUSES, AND SOME ARE FOR FIGHTING PARASITES.

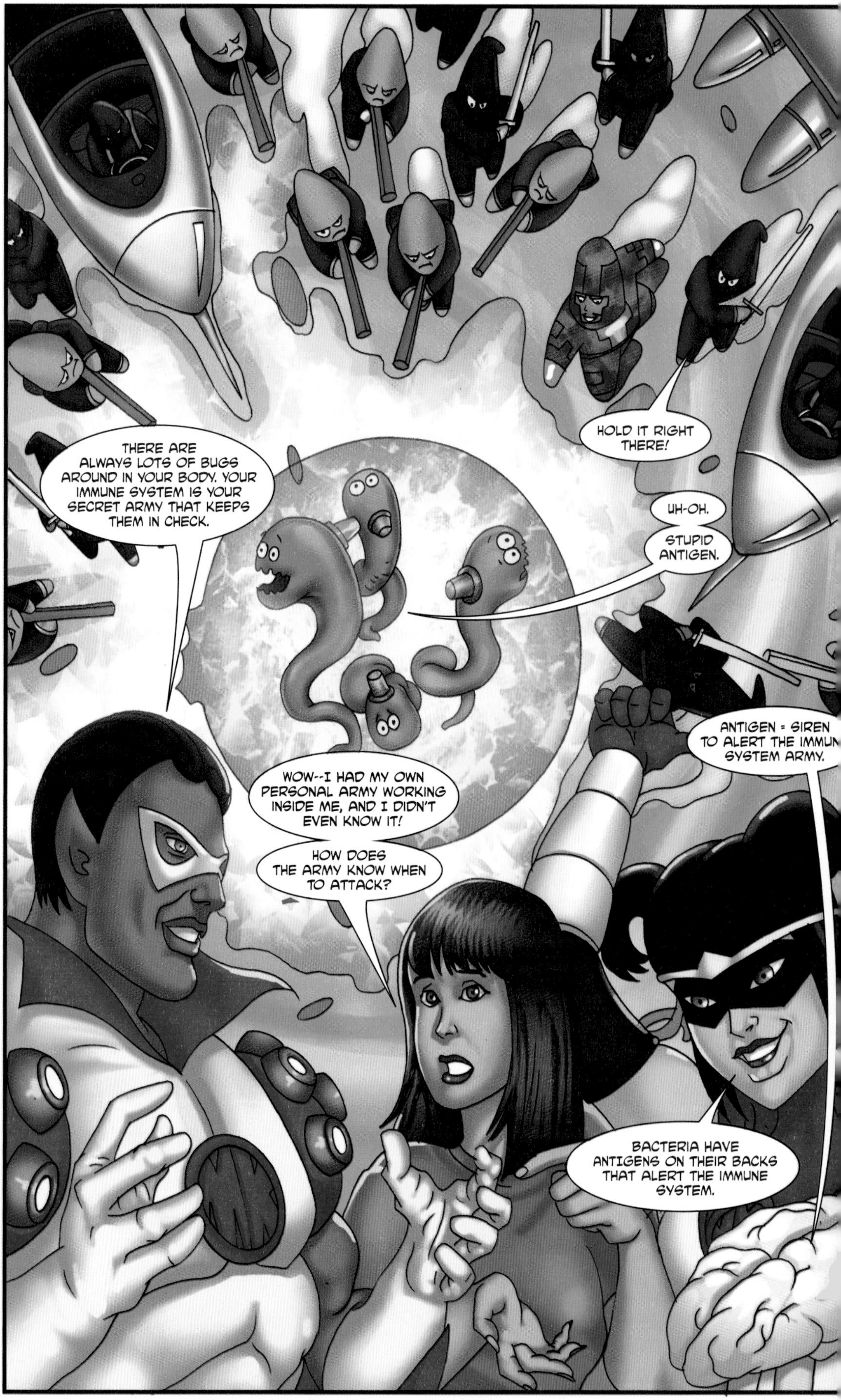
THERE ARE ALWAYS LOTS OF BUGS AROUND IN YOUR BODY. YOUR IMMUNE SYSTEM IS YOUR SECRET ARMY THAT KEEPS THEM IN CHECK.
HOLD IT RIGHT THERE!
UH-OH.
STUPID ANTIGEN.
WOW--I HAD MY OWN PERSONAL ARMY WORKING INSIDE ME, AND I DIDN'T EVEN KNOW IT!
HOW DOES THE ARMY KNOW WHEN TO ATTACK?
ANTIGEN = SIREN TO ALERT THE IMMUN SYSTEM ARMY.
BACTERIA HAVE ANTIGENS ON THEIR BACKS THAT ALERT THE IMMUNE SYSTEM.

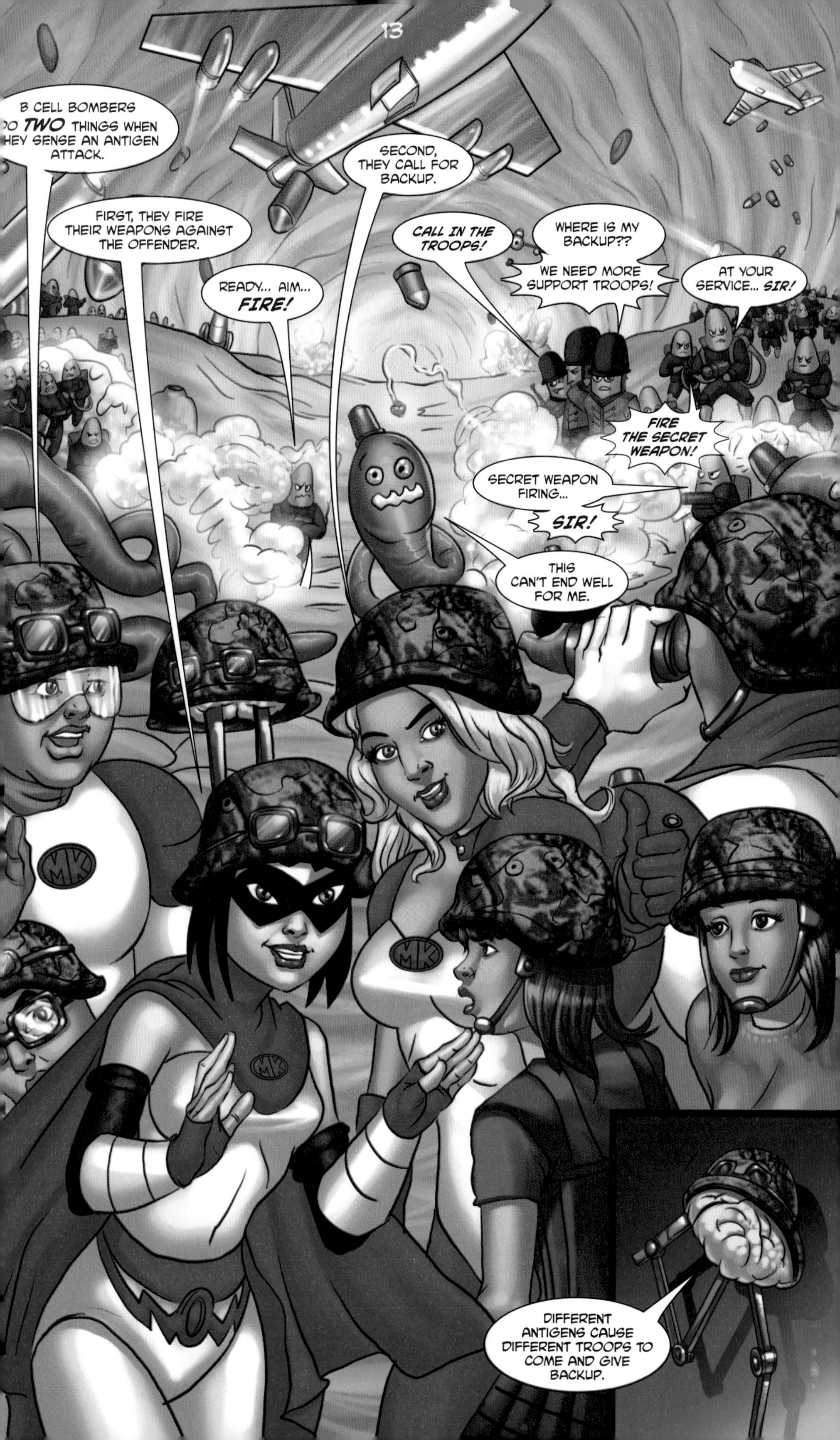
B CELL BOMBERS DO TWO THINGS WHEN THEY SENSE AN ANTIGEN ATTACK.
FIRST, THEY FIRE THEIR WEAPONS AGAINST THE OFFENDER.
READY... AIM... FIRE!
SECOND, THEY CALL FOR BACKUP.
CALL IN THE TROOPS!
WHERE IS MY BACKUP??
WE NEED MORE SUPPORT TROOPS!
AT YOUR SERVICE... SIR!
FIRE THE SECRET WEAPON!
SECRET WEAPON FIRING...
SIR!
THIS CAN'T END WELL FOR ME.
DIFFERENT ANTIGENS CAUSE DIFFERENT TROOPS TO COME AND GIVE BACKUP.

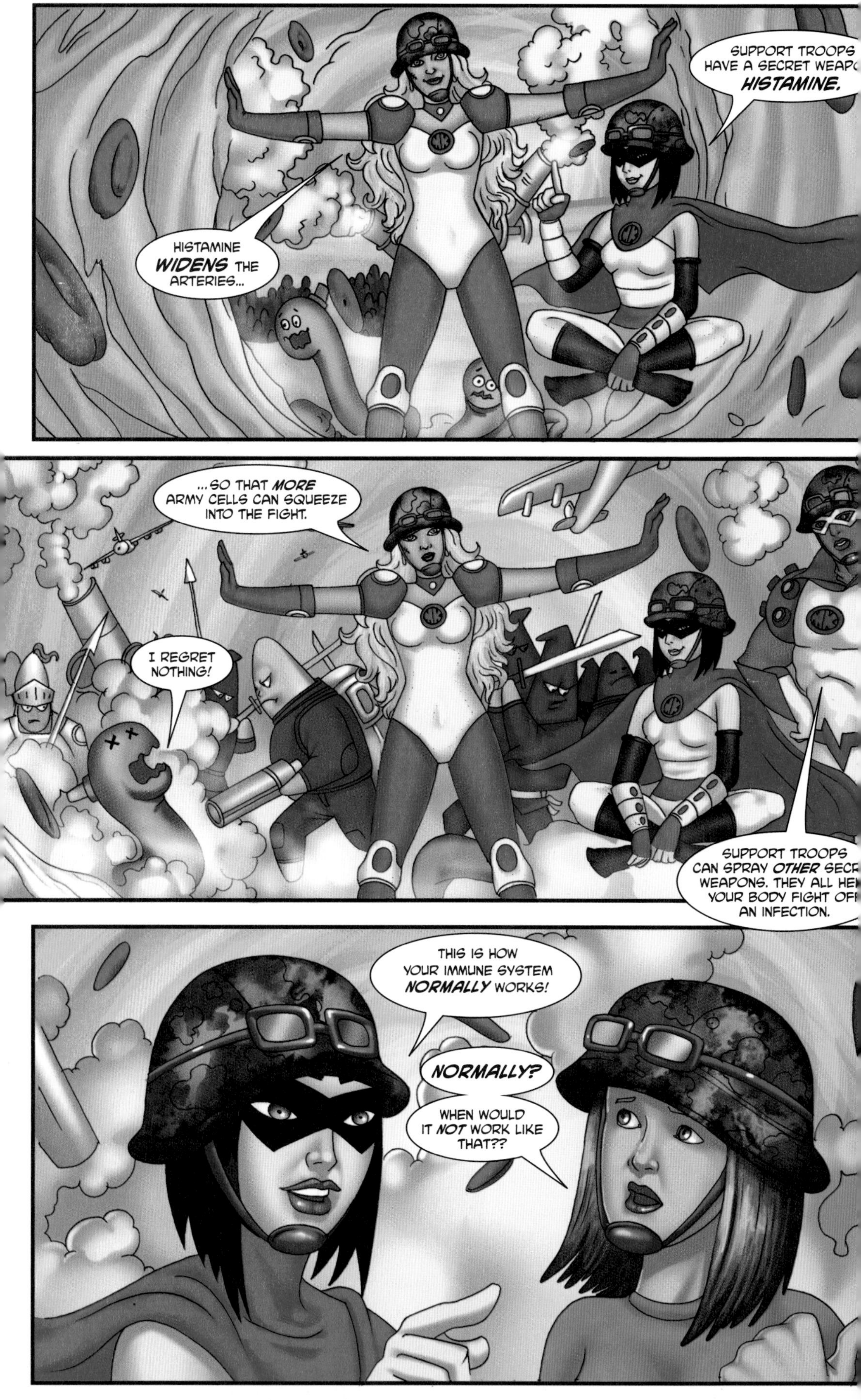
SUPPORT TROOPS HAVE A SECRET WEAPO
HISTAMINE.
HISTAMINE WIDENS THE ARTERIES...
...SO THAT MORE ARMY CELLS CAN SQUEEZE INTO THE FIGHT.
I REGRET NOTHING!
SUPPORT TROOPS CAN SPRAY OTHER SECR WEAPONS. THEY ALL HE YOUR BODY FIGHT OF AN INFECTION.
THIS IS HOW YOUR IMMUNE SYSTEM NORMALLY WORKS!
NORMALLY?
WHEN WOULD IT NOT WORK LIKE THAT??

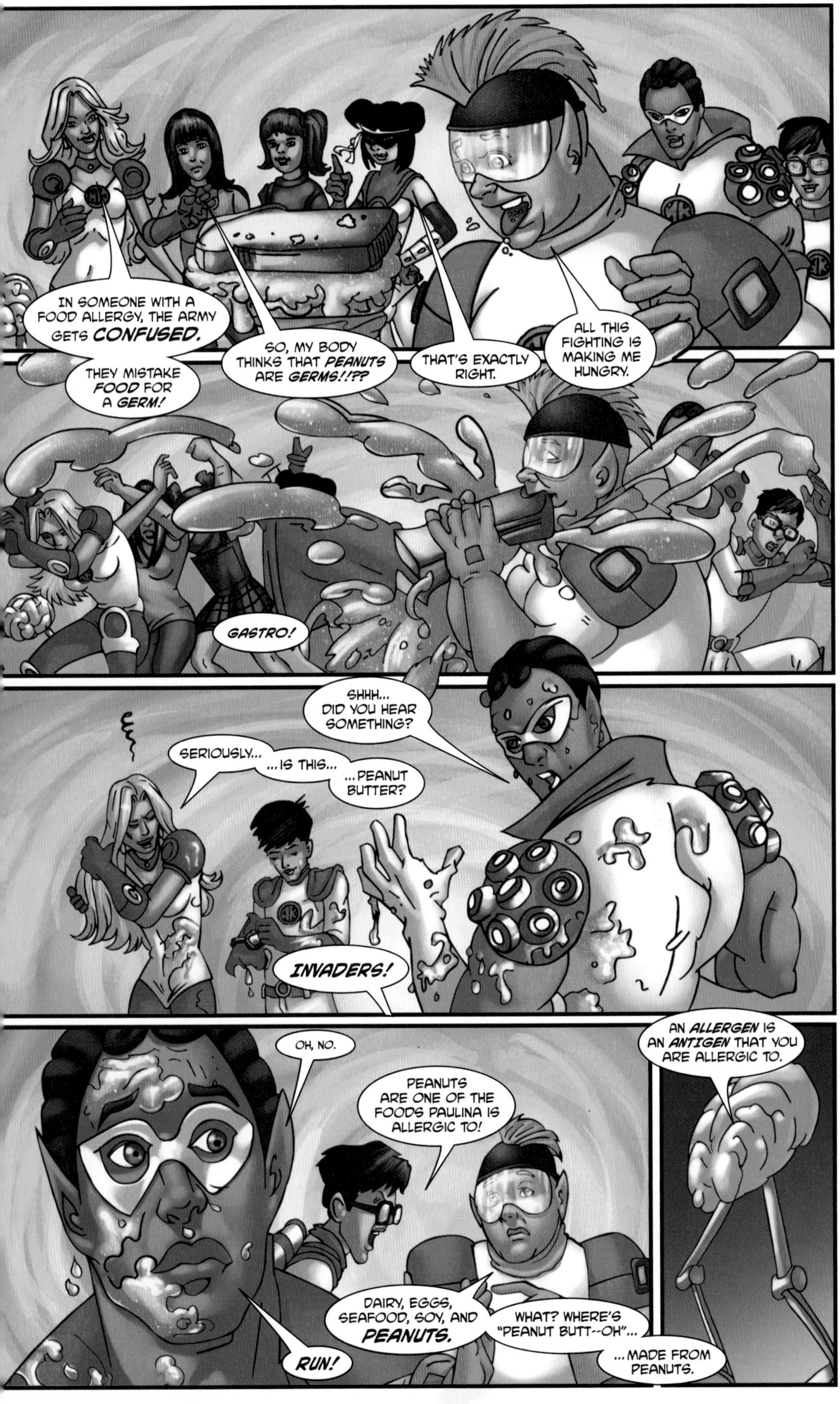
IN SOMEONE WITH A FOOD ALLERGY, THE ARMY GETS CONFUSED.
THEY MISTAKE FOOD FOR A GERM!
SO, MY BODY THINKS THAT PEANUTS ARE GERMS!!??
THAT'S EXACTLY RIGHT.
ALL THIS FIGHTING IS MAKING ME HUNGRY.
GASTRO!
SHHH... DID YOU HEAR SOMETHING?
SERIOUSLY...
...IS THIS...
...PEANUT BUTTER?
INVADERS!
OH, NO.
PEANUTS ARE ONE OF THE FOODS PAULINA IS ALLERGIC TO!
AN ALLERGEN IS AN ANTIGEN THAT YOU ARE ALLERGIC TO.
RUN!
DAIRY, EGGS, SEAFOOD, SOY, AND PEANUTS.
WHAT? WHERE'S "PEANUT BUTT--OH"...
...MADE FROM PEANUTS.

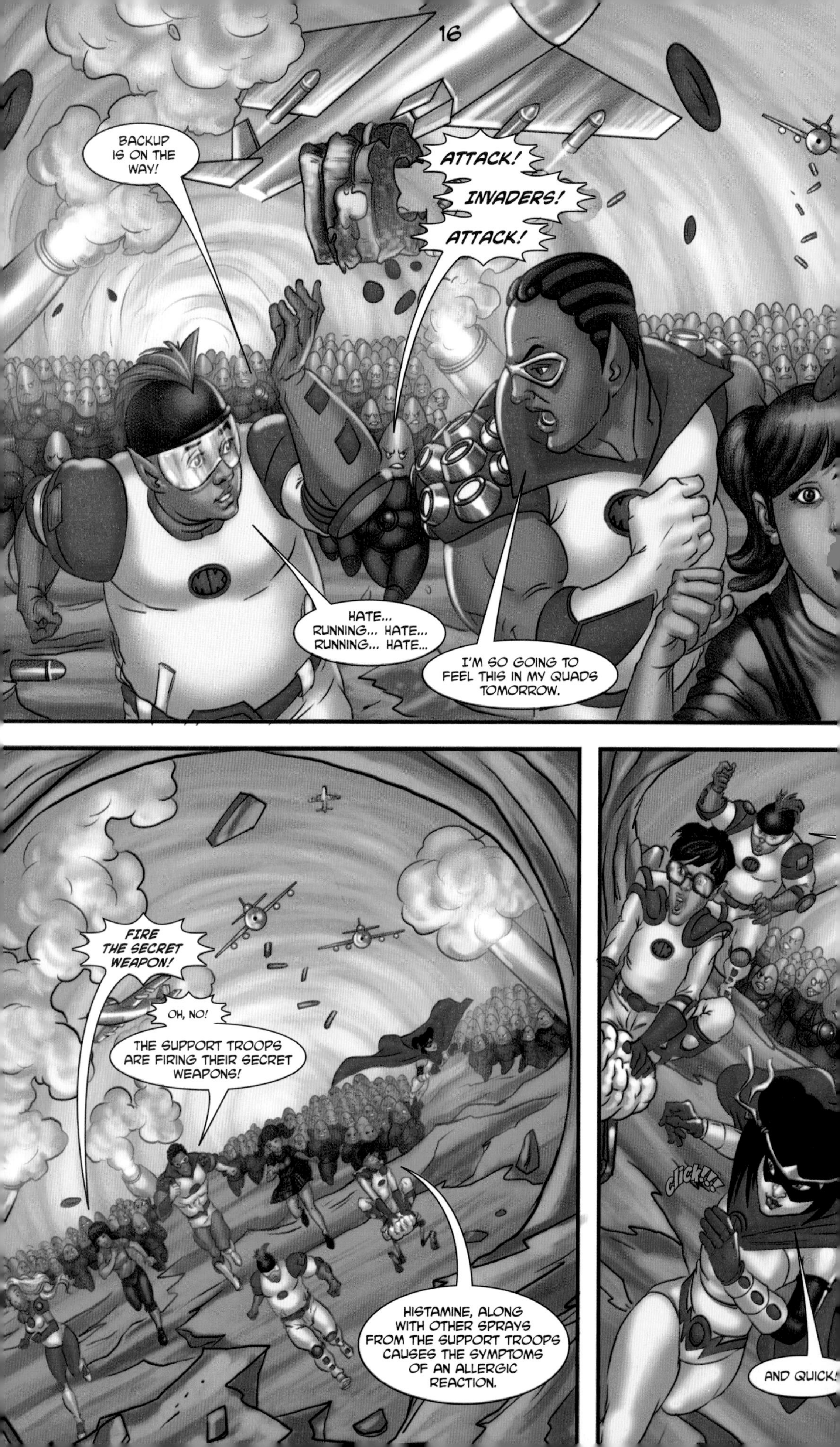
BACKUP IS ON THE WAY!
ATTACK!
INVADERS!
ATTACK!
HATE... RUNNING... HATE... RUNNING... HATE...
I'M SO GOING TO FEEL THIS IN MY QUADS TOMORROW.
FIRE THE SECRET WEAPON!
OH, NO!
THE SUPPORT TROOPS ARE FIRING THEIR SECRET WEAPONS!
HISTAMINE, ALONG WITH OTHER SPRAYS FROM THE SUPPORT TROOPS CAUSES THE SYMPTOMS OF AN ALLERGIC REACTION.
click!!!
AND QUICK!

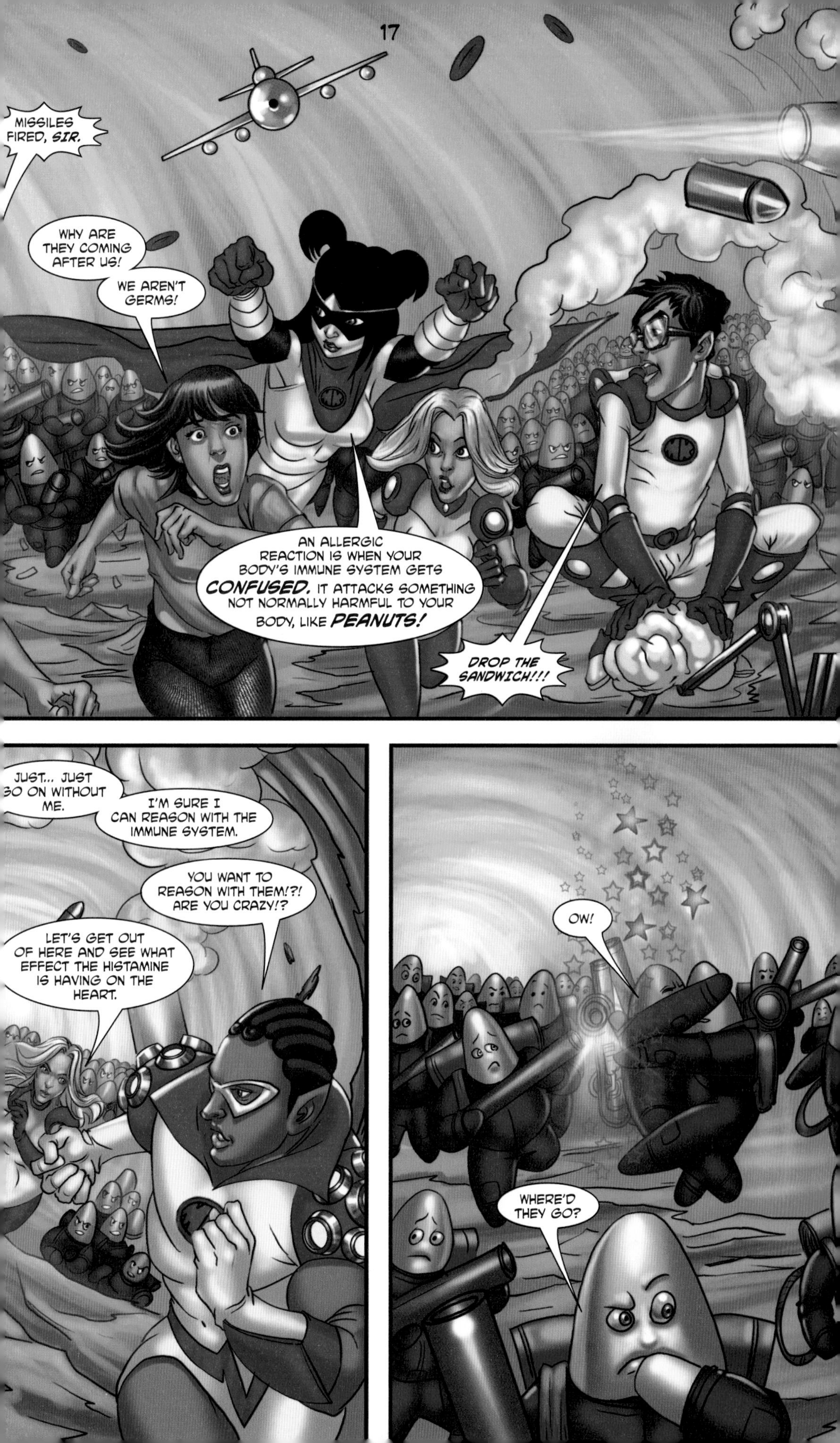
MISSILES FIRED, SIR.
WHY ARE THEY COMING AFTER US!
WE AREN'T GERMS!
AN ALLERGIC REACTION IS WHEN YOUR BODY'S IMMUNE SYSTEM GETS CONFUSED. IT ATTACKS SOMETHING NOT NORMALLY HARMFUL TO YOUR BODY, LIKE PEANUTS!
DROP THE SANDWICH!!!
JUST... JUST GO ON WITHOUT ME.
I'M SURE I CAN REASON WITH THE IMMUNE SYSTEM.
YOU WANT TO REASON WITH THEM!?! ARE YOU CRAZY!?
LET'S GET OUT OF HERE AND SEE WHAT EFFECT THE HISTAMINE IS HAVING ON THE HEART.
OW!
WHERE'D THEY GO?

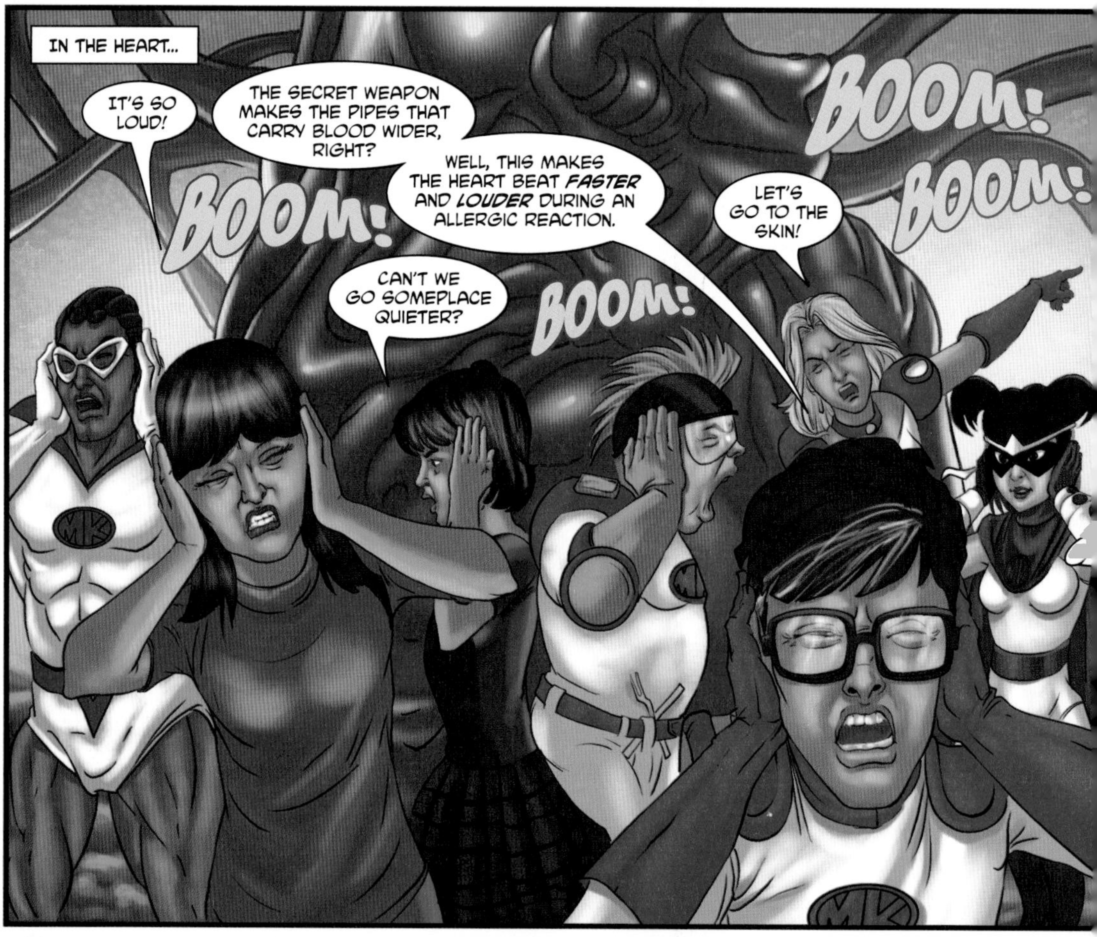
IN THE HEART...
IT'S SO LOUD!
THE SECRET WEAPON MAKES THE PIPES THAT CARRY BLOOD WIDER, RIGHT?
BOOM!
WELL, THIS MAKES THE HEART BEAT FASTER AND LOUDER DURING AN ALLERGIC REACTION.
BOOM!
LET'S GO TO THE SKIN!
BOOM!
BOOM!
CAN'T WE GO SOMEPLACE QUIETER?

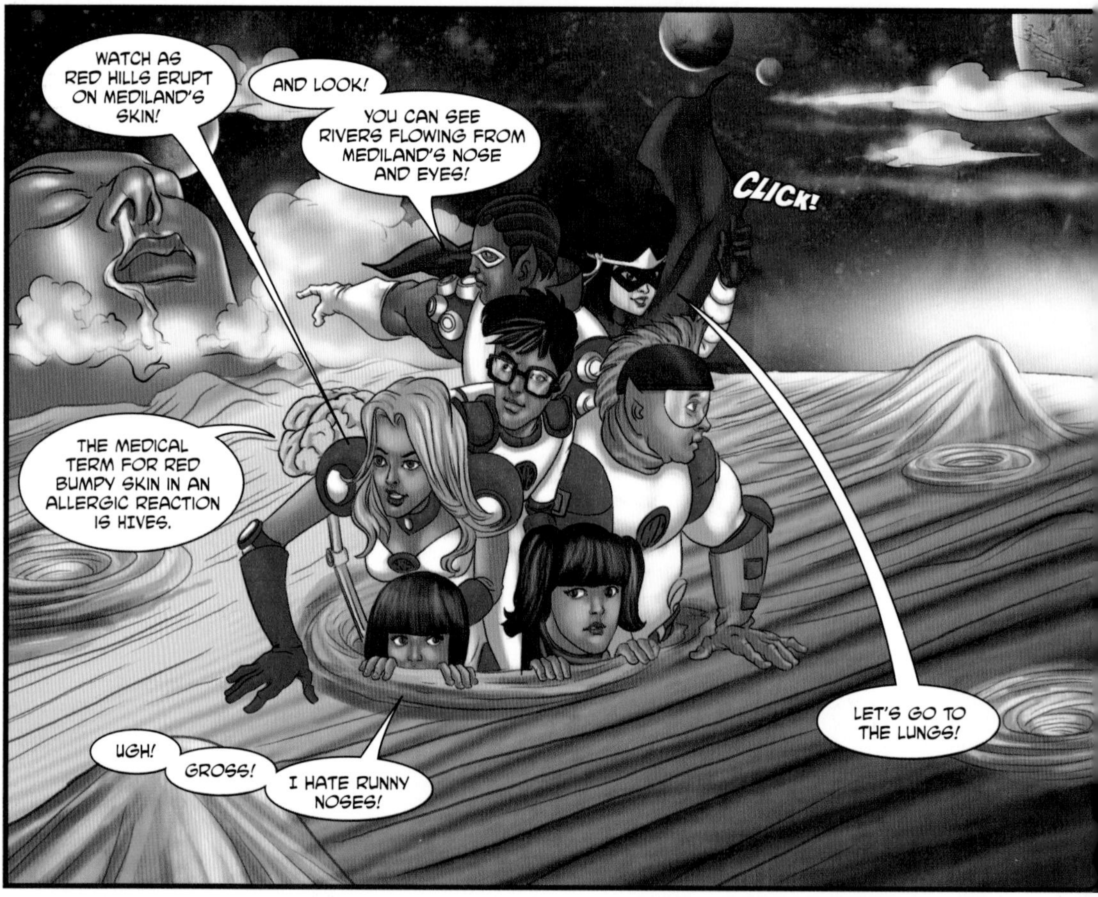
WATCH AS RED HILLS ERUPT ON MEDILAND'S SKIN!
AND LOOK!
YOU CAN SEE RIVERS FLOWING FROM MEDILAND'S NOSE AND EYES!
CLICK!
THE MEDICAL TERM FOR RED BUMPY SKIN IN AN ALLERGIC REACTION IS HIVES.
LET'S GO TO THE LUNGS!
UGH!
GROSS!
I HATE RUNNY NOSES!

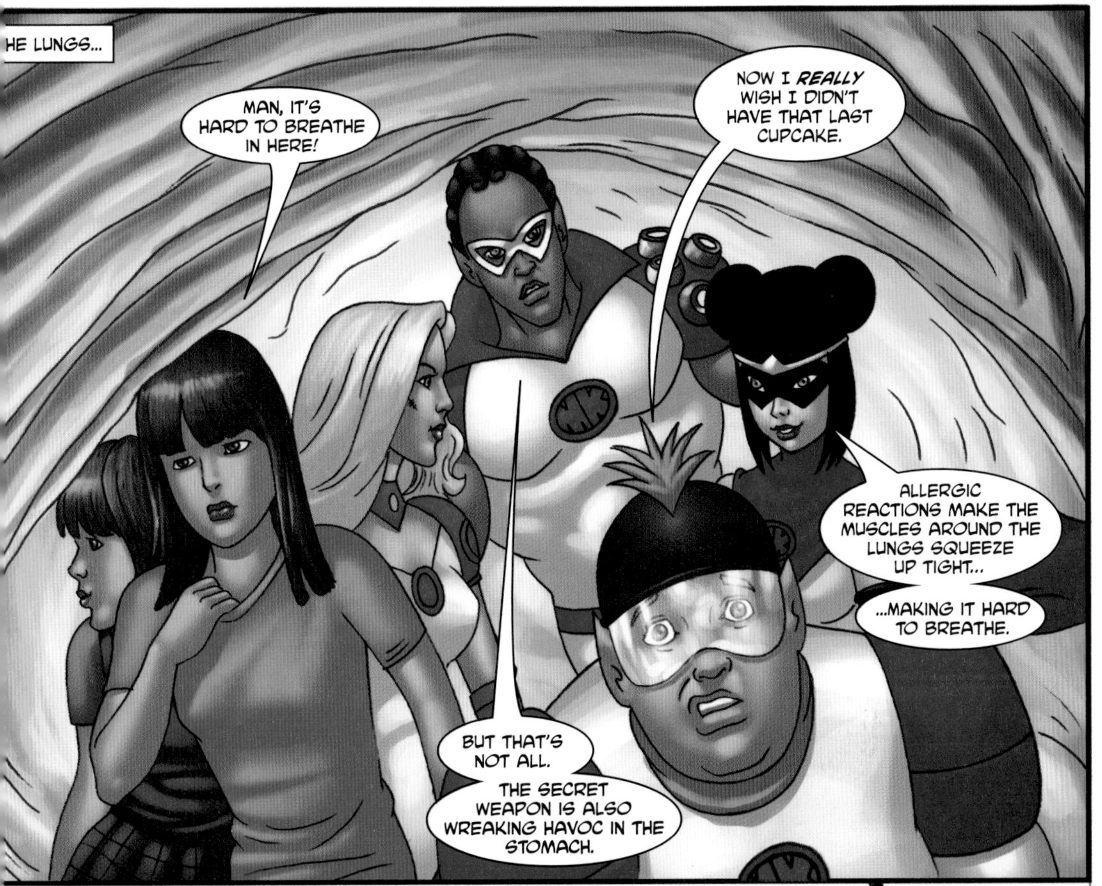
HE LUNGS...
MAN, IT'S HARD TO BREATHE IN HERE!
NOW I *REALLY* WISH I DIDN'T HAVE THAT LAST CUPCAKE.
ALLERGIC REACTIONS MAKE THE MUSCLES AROUND THE LUNGS SQUEEZE UP TIGHT...
...MAKING IT HARD TO BREATHE.
BUT THAT'S NOT ALL.
THE SECRET WEAPON IS ALSO WREAKING HAVOC IN THE STOMACH.

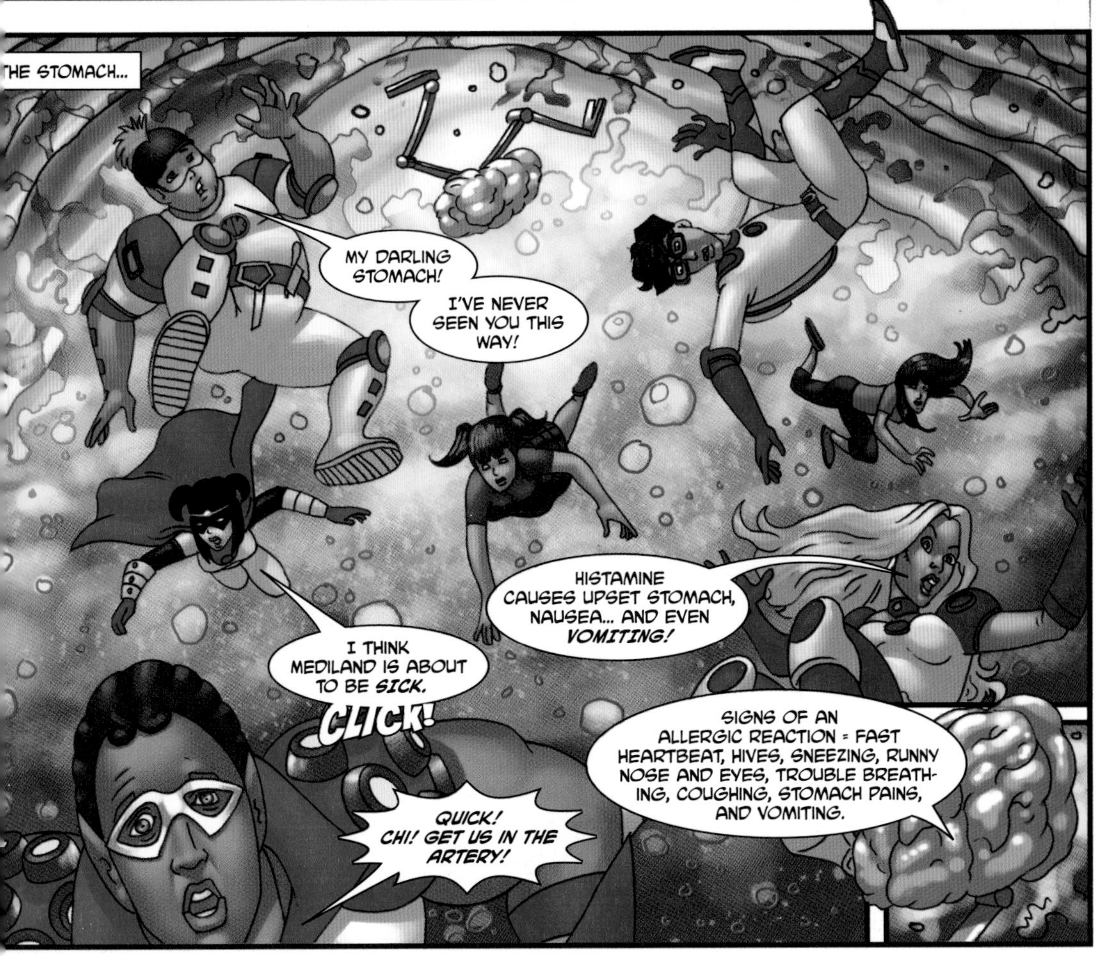
THE STOMACH...
MY DARLING STOMACH!
I'VE NEVER SEEN YOU THIS WAY!
HISTAMINE CAUSES UPSET STOMACH, NAUSEA... AND EVEN *VOMITING!*
I THINK MEDILAND IS ABOUT TO BE *SICK*.
CLICK!
SIGNS OF AN ALLERGIC REACTION = FAST HEARTBEAT, HIVES, SNEEZING, RUNNY NOSE AND EYES, TROUBLE BREATHING, COUGHING, STOMACH PAINS, AND VOMITING.
QUICK! CHI! GET US IN THE ARTERY!

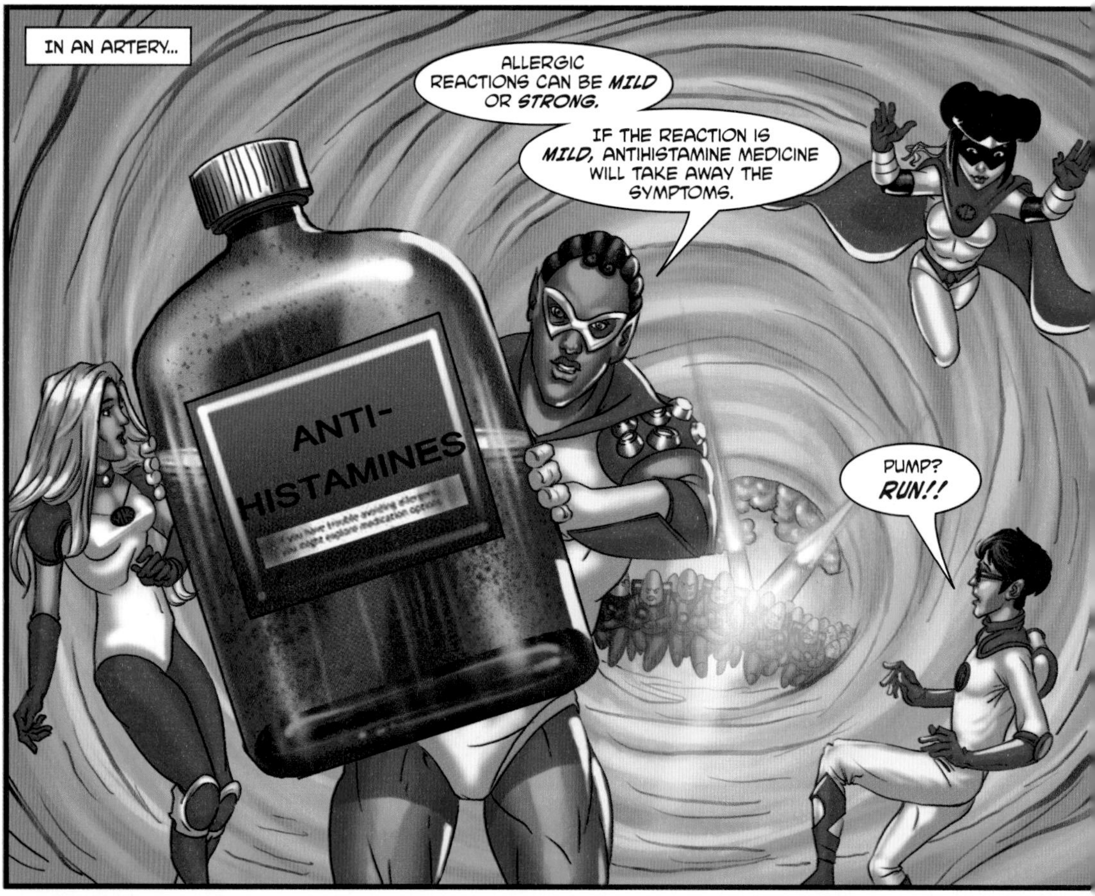
IN AN ARTERY...
ALLERGIC REACTIONS CAN BE *MILD* OR *STRONG.*
IF THE REACTION IS *MILD,* ANTIHISTAMINE MEDICINE WILL TAKE AWAY THE SYMPTOMS.
ANTI-HISTAMINES
PUMP? *RUN!!*

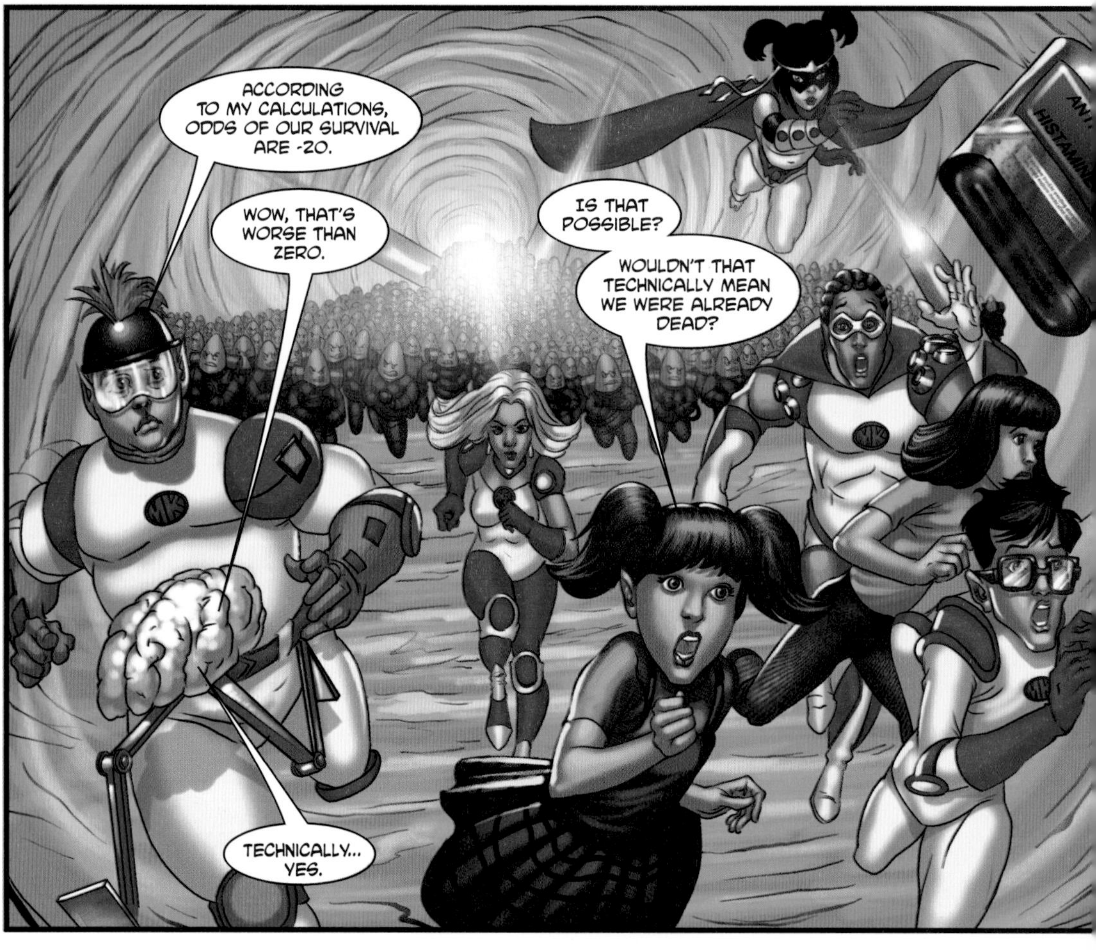
ACCORDING TO MY CALCULATIONS, ODDS OF OUR SURVIVAL ARE -20.
WOW, THAT'S WORSE THAN ZERO.
IS THAT POSSIBLE?
WOULDN'T THAT TECHNICALLY MEAN WE WERE ALREADY DEAD?
TECHNICALLY... YES.

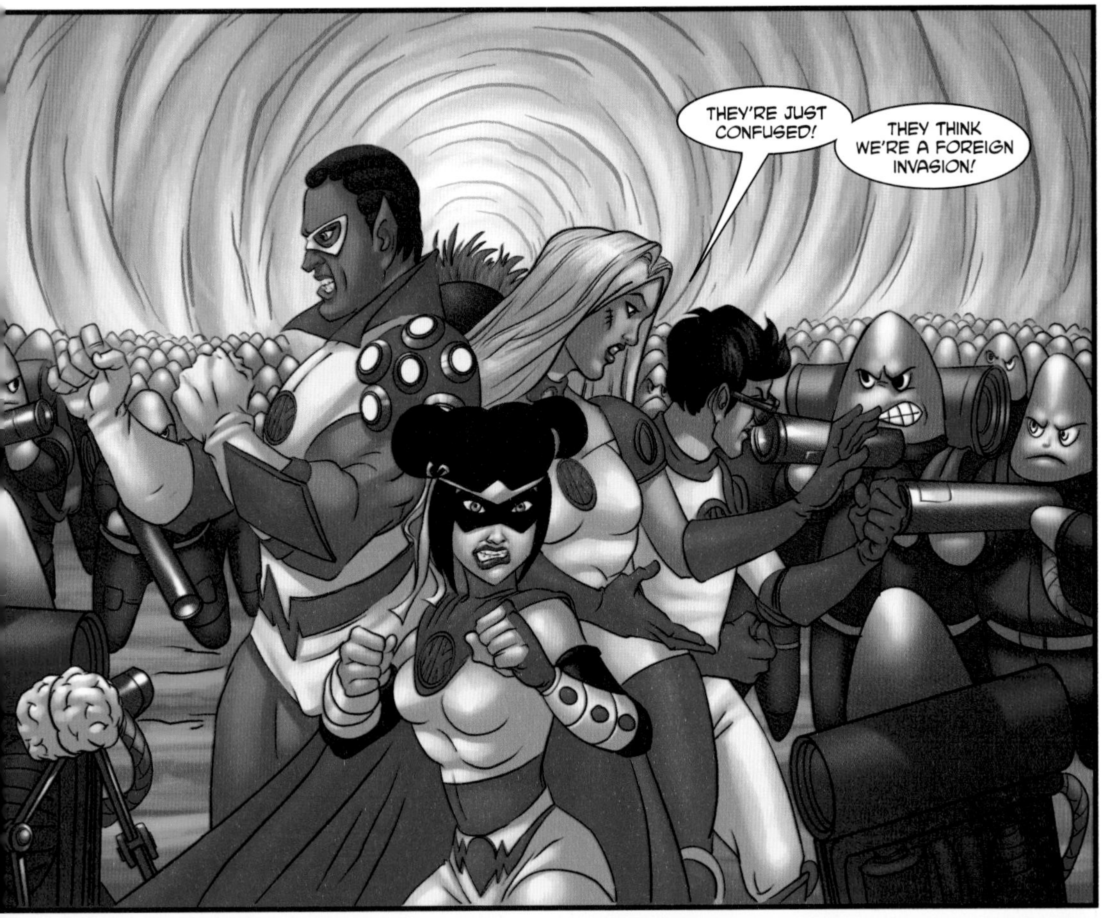
THEY'RE JUST CONFUSED!
THEY THINK WE'RE A FOREIGN INVASION!

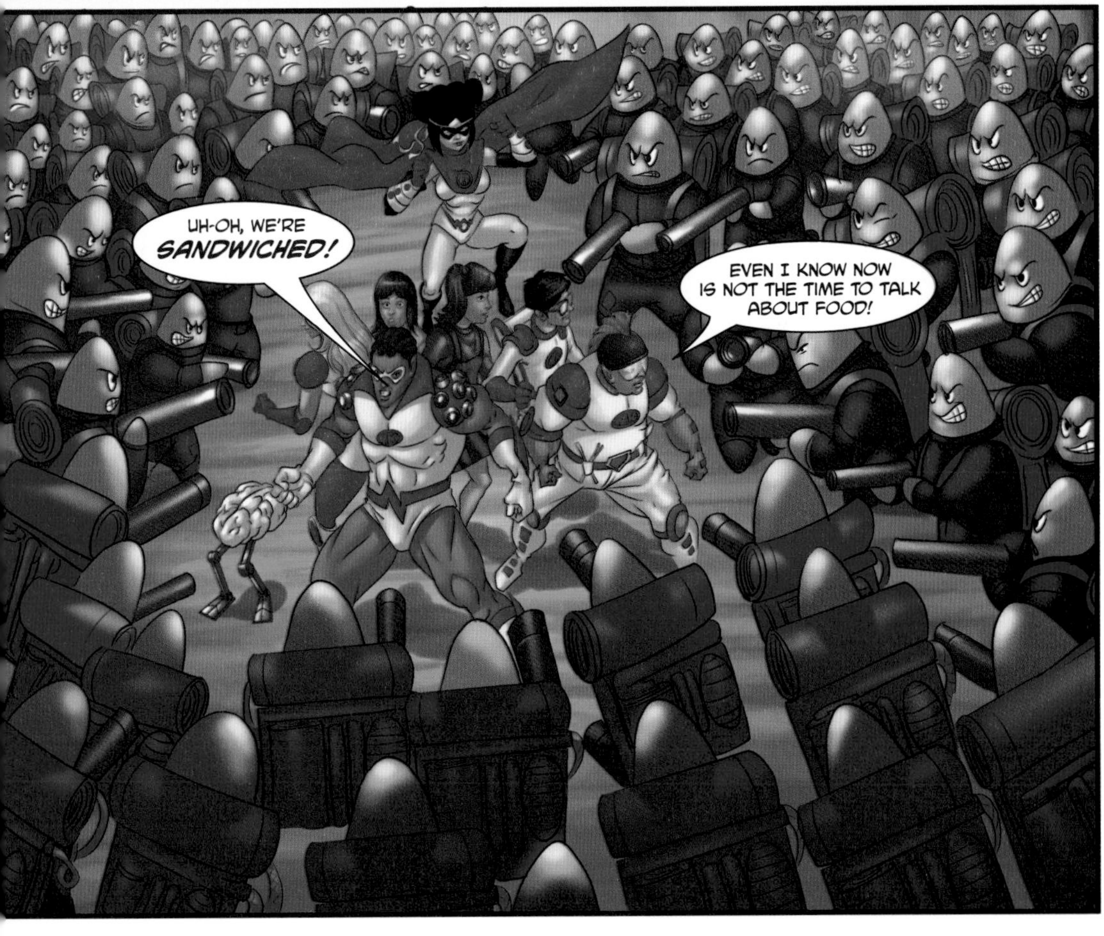
UH-OH, WE'RE SANDWICHED!
EVEN I KNOW NOW IS NOT THE TIME TO TALK ABOUT FOOD!

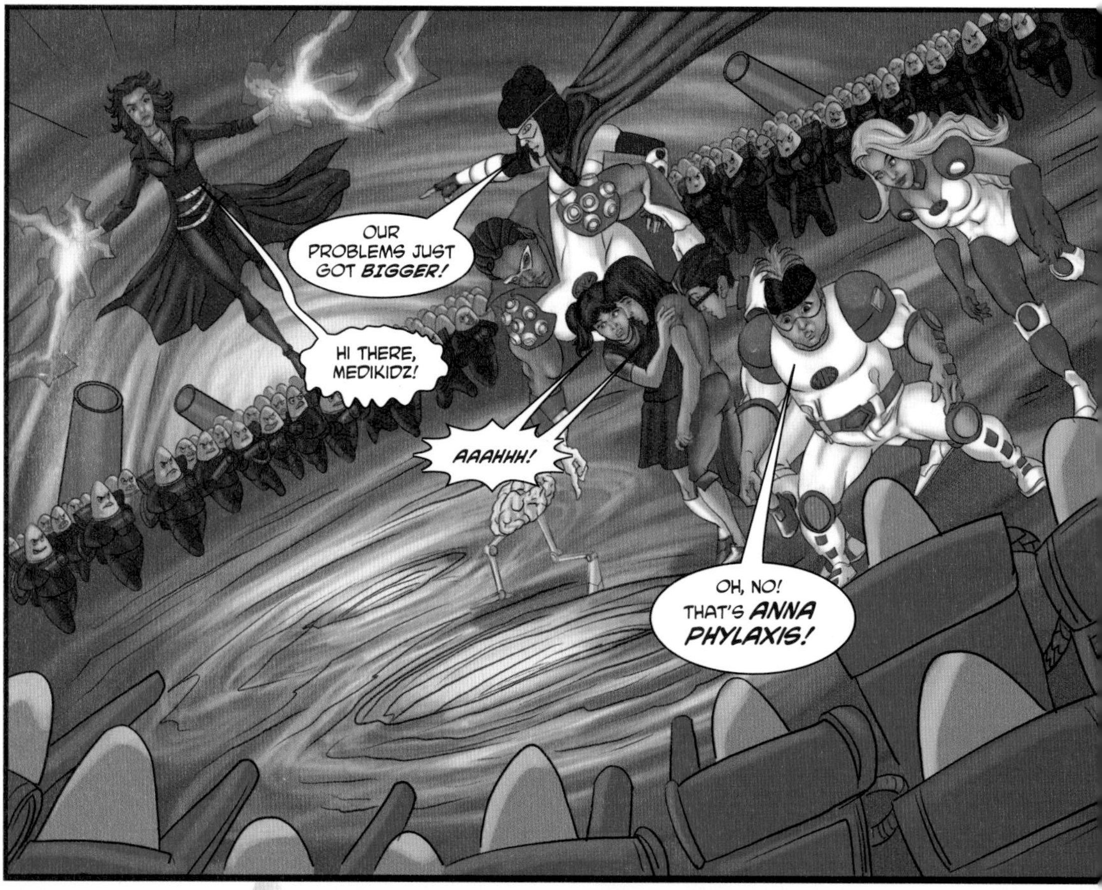
OUR PROBLEMS JUST GOT BIGGER!
HI THERE, MEDIKIDZ!
AAAHHH!
OH, NO! THAT'S ANNA PHYLAXIS!

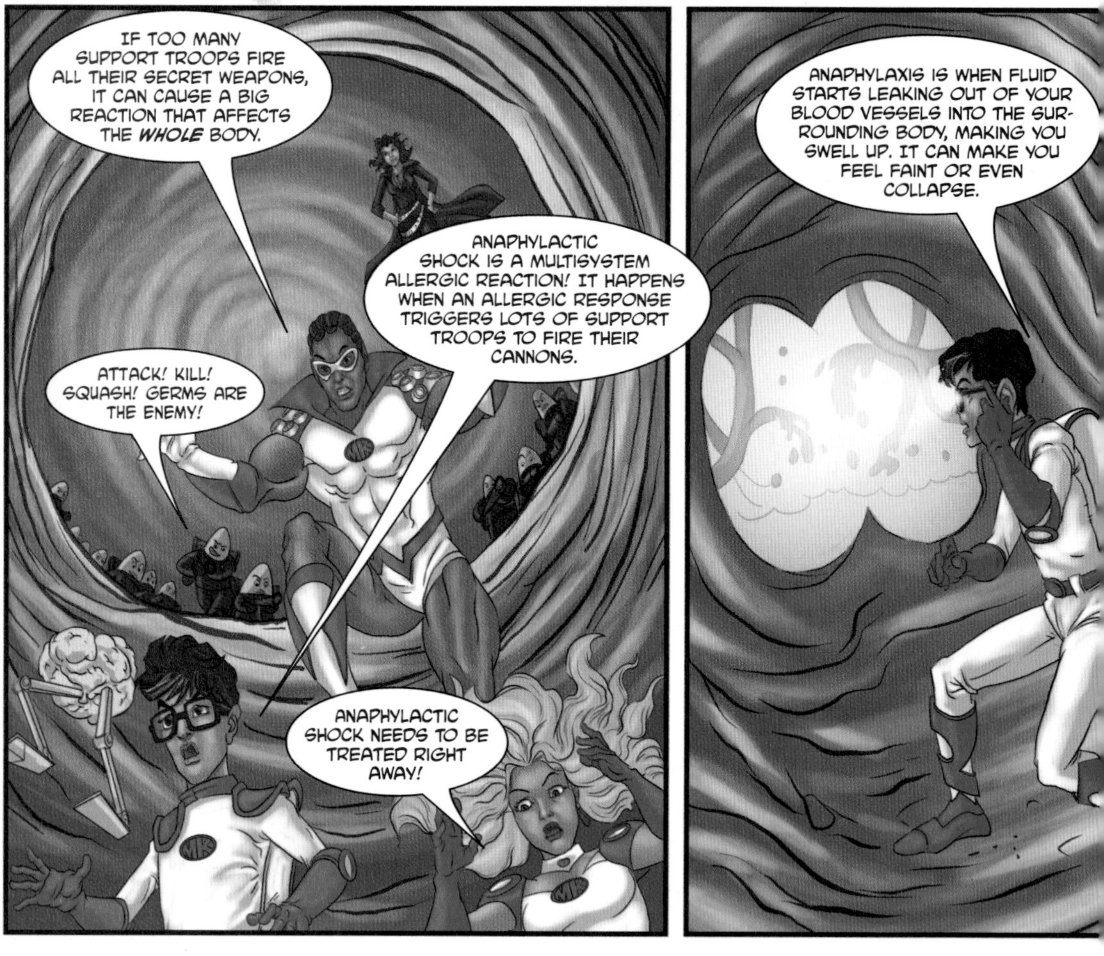
IF TOO MANY SUPPORT TROOPS FIRE ALL THEIR SECRET WEAPONS, IT CAN CAUSE A BIG REACTION THAT AFFECTS THE WHOLE BODY.
ANAPHYLACTIC SHOCK IS A MULTISYSTEM ALLERGIC REACTION! IT HAPPENS WHEN AN ALLERGIC RESPONSE TRIGGERS LOTS OF SUPPORT TROOPS TO FIRE THEIR CANNONS.
ATTACK! KILL! SQUASH! GERMS ARE THE ENEMY!
ANAPHYLACTIC SHOCK NEEDS TO BE TREATED RIGHT AWAY!
ANAPHYLAXIS IS WHEN FLUID STARTS LEAKING OUT OF YOUR BLOOD VESSELS INTO THE SUR-ROUNDING BODY, MAKING YOU SWELL UP. IT CAN MAKE YOU FEEL FAINT OR EVEN COLLAPSE.

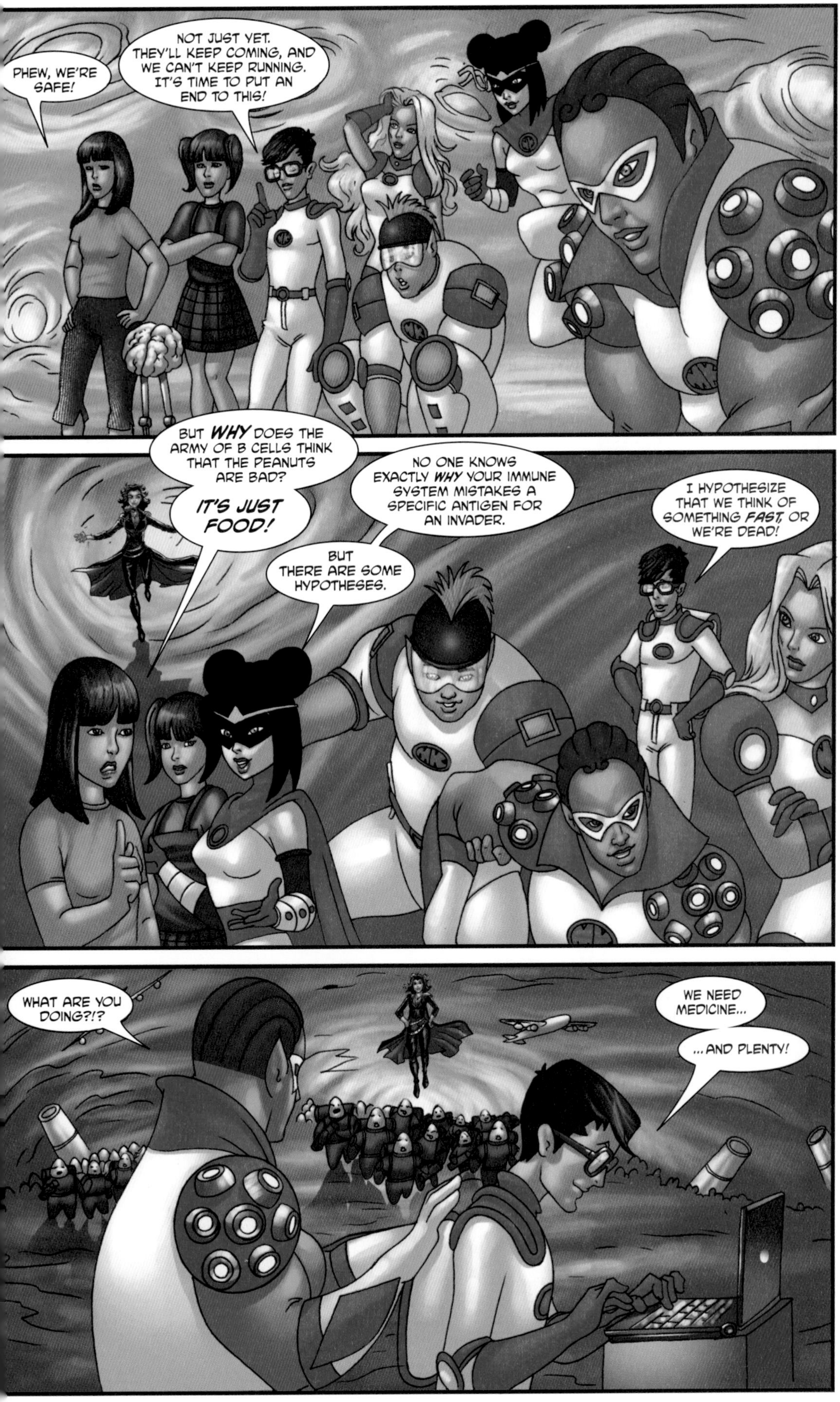
PHEW, WE'RE SAFE!
NOT JUST YET. THEY'LL KEEP COMING, AND WE CAN'T KEEP RUNNING. IT'S TIME TO PUT AN END TO THIS!
BUT WHY DOES THE ARMY OF B CELLS THINK THAT THE PEANUTS ARE BAD?
IT'S JUST FOOD!
NO ONE KNOWS EXACTLY WHY YOUR IMMUNE SYSTEM MISTAKES A SPECIFIC ANTIGEN FOR AN INVADER.
BUT THERE ARE SOME HYPOTHESES.
I HYPOTHESIZE THAT WE THINK OF SOMETHING FAST, OR WE'RE DEAD!
WHAT ARE YOU DOING?!?
WE NEED MEDICINE...
...AND PLENTY!

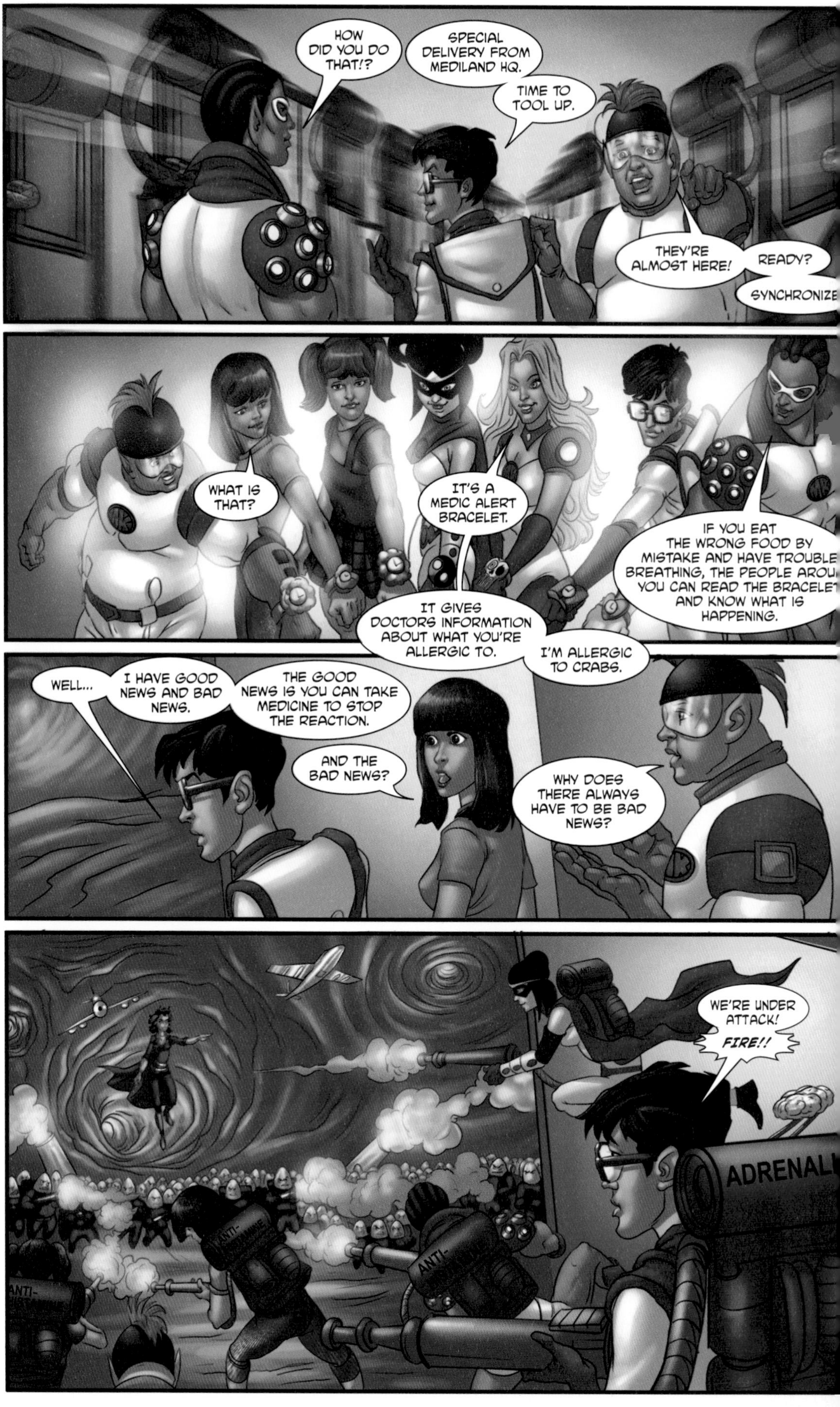
HOW DID YOU DO THAT!?
SPECIAL DELIVERY FROM MEDILAND HQ.
TIME TO TOOL UP.
THEY'RE ALMOST HERE!
READY?
SYNCHRONIZE
WHAT IS THAT?
IT'S A MEDIC ALERT BRACELET.
IT GIVES DOCTORS INFORMATION ABOUT WHAT YOU'RE ALLERGIC TO.
IF YOU EAT THE WRONG FOOD BY MISTAKE AND HAVE TROUBLE BREATHING, THE PEOPLE AROU YOU CAN READ THE BRACELET AND KNOW WHAT IS HAPPENING.
I'M ALLERGIC TO CRABS.
WELL...
I HAVE GOOD NEWS AND BAD NEWS.
THE GOOD NEWS IS YOU CAN TAKE MEDICINE TO STOP THE REACTION.
AND THE BAD NEWS?
WHY DOES THERE ALWAYS HAVE TO BE BAD NEWS?
WE'RE UNDER ATTACK!
FIRE!!
ANTI-
ANTI-
ADRENALI

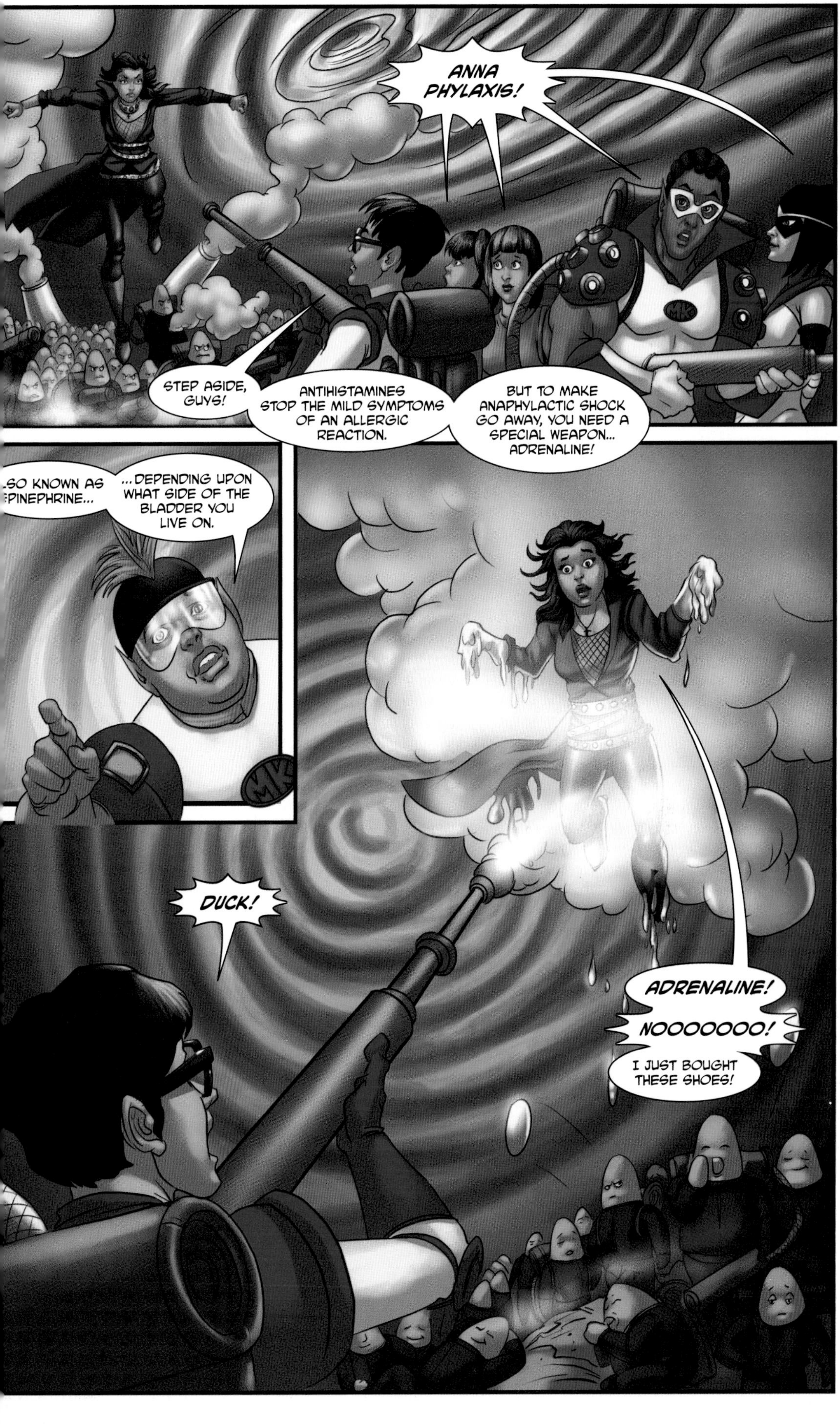
ANNA PHYLAXIS!
STEP ASIDE, GUYS!
ANTIHISTAMINES STOP THE MILD SYMPTOMS OF AN ALLERGIC REACTION.
BUT TO MAKE ANAPHYLACTIC SHOCK GO AWAY, YOU NEED A SPECIAL WEAPON... ADRENALINE!
...DEPENDING UPON WHAT SIDE OF THE BLADDER YOU LIVE ON.
DUCK!
ADRENALINE!
NOOOOOOO!
I JUST BOUGHT THESE SHOES!

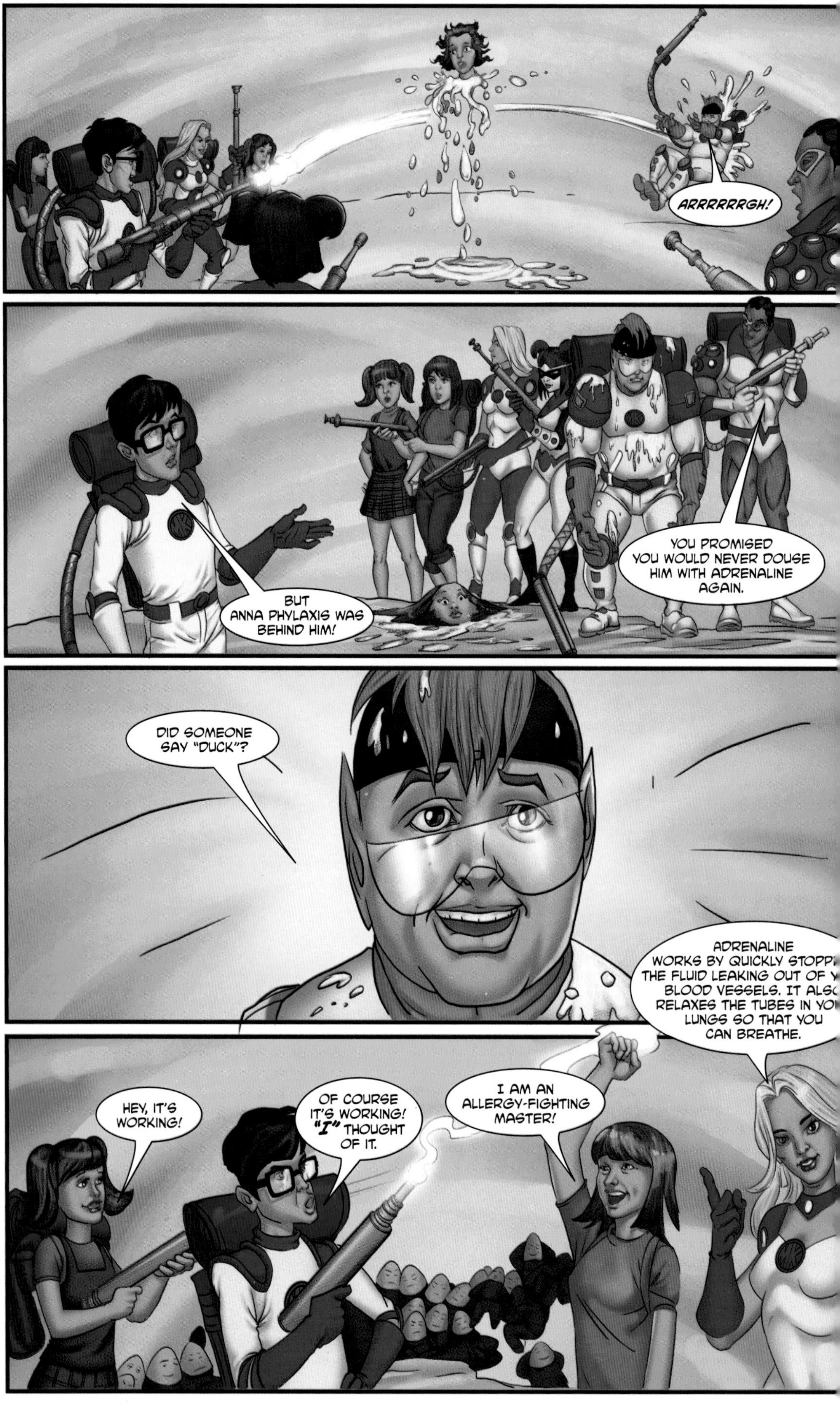
ARRRRRRGH!
BUT ANNA PHYLAXIS WAS BEHIND HIM!
YOU PROMISED YOU WOULD NEVER DOUSE HIM WITH ADRENALINE AGAIN.
DID SOMEONE SAY "DUCK"?
ADRENALINE WORKS BY QUICKLY STOPP THE FLUID LEAKING OUT OF Y BLOOD VESSELS. IT ALS RELAXES THE TUBES IN YO LUNGS SO THAT YOU CAN BREATHE.
HEY, IT'S WORKING!
OF COURSE IT'S WORKING! "I" THOUGHT OF IT.
I AM AN ALLERGY-FIGHTING MASTER!

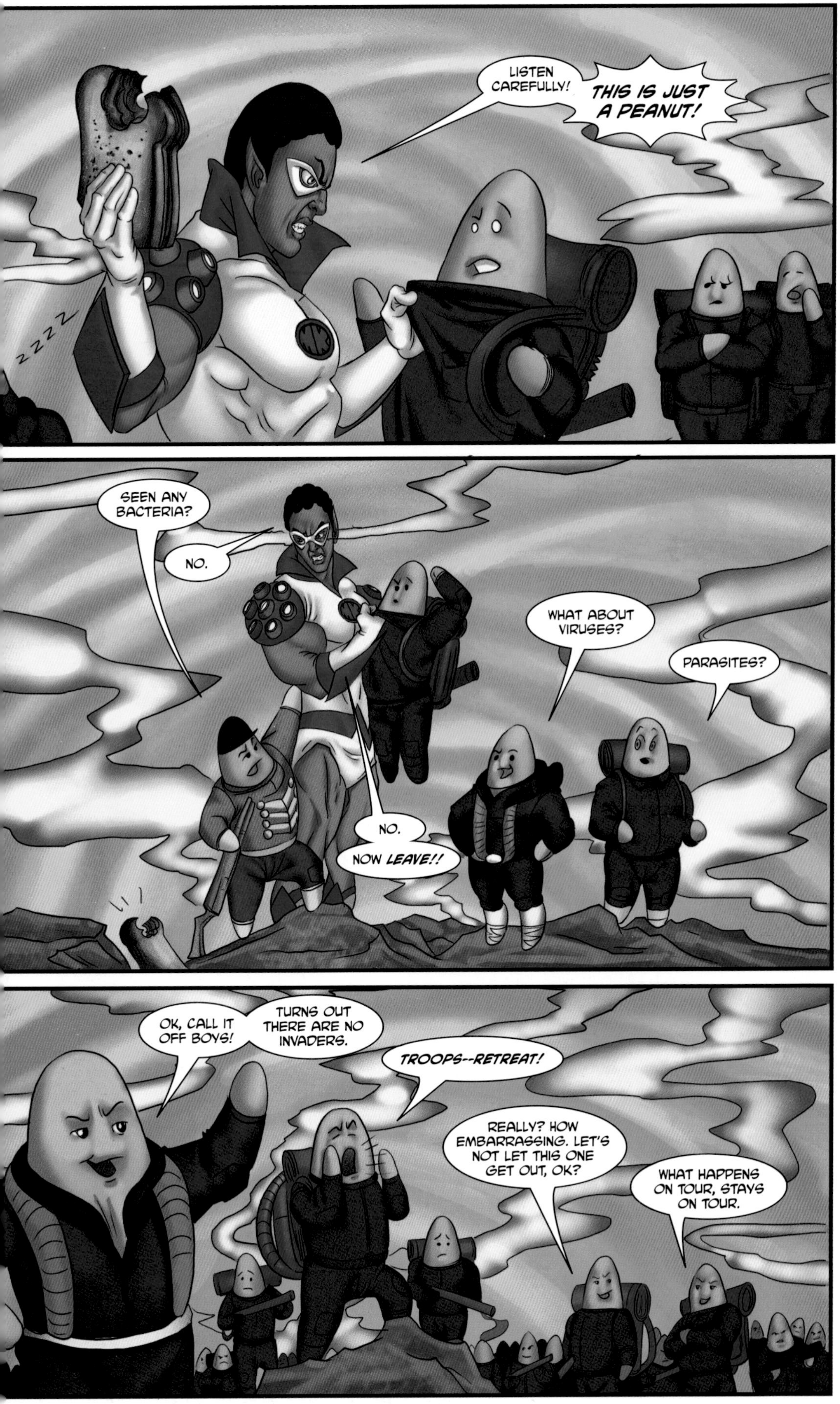
LISTEN CAREFULLY!
THIS IS JUST A PEANUT!
ZZZZ
SEEN ANY BACTERIA?
NO.
WHAT ABOUT VIRUSES?
PARASITES?
NO.
NOW *LEAVE!!*
OK, CALL IT OFF BOYS!
TURNS OUT THERE ARE NO INVADERS.
TROOPS--RETREAT!
REALLY? HOW EMBARRASSING. LET'S NOT LET THIS ONE GET OUT, OK?
WHAT HAPPENS ON TOUR, STAYS ON TOUR.

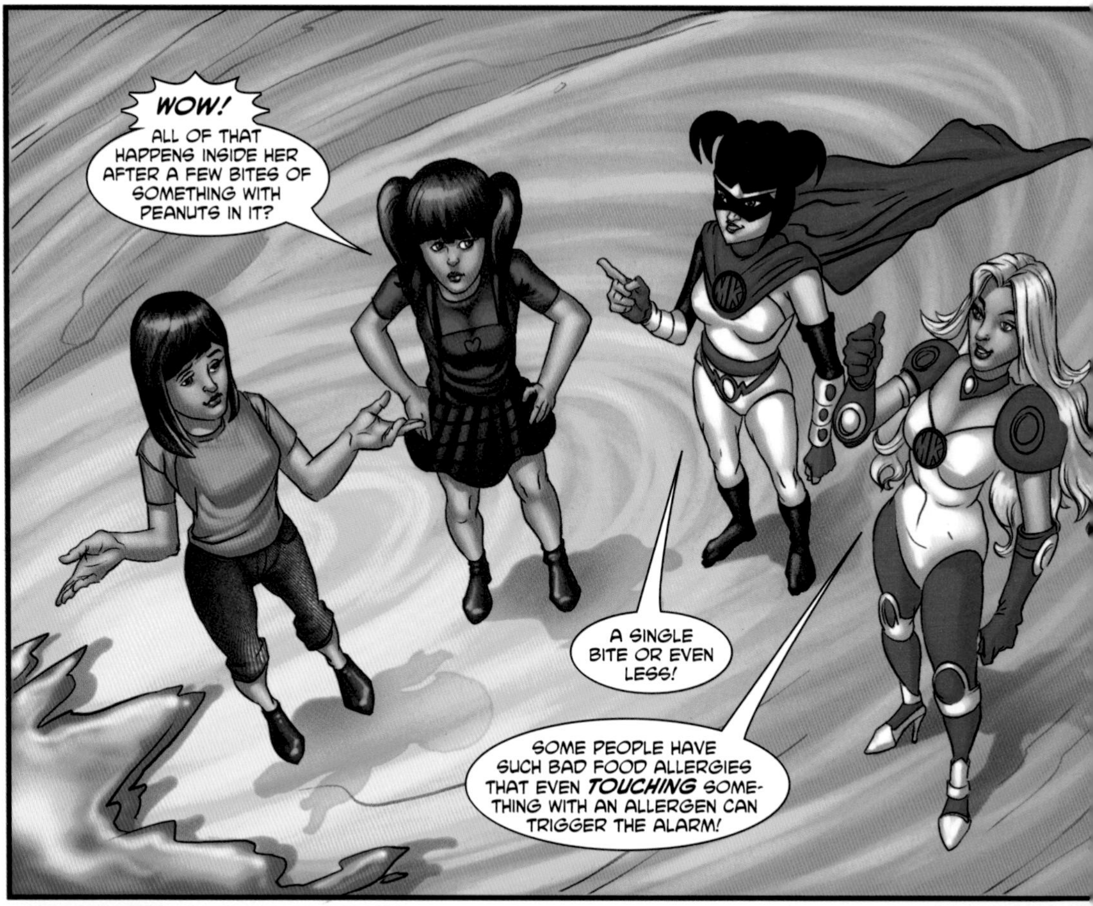
WOW!
ALL OF THAT HAPPENS INSIDE HER AFTER A FEW BITES OF SOMETHING WITH PEANUTS IN IT?
A SINGLE BITE OR EVEN LESS!
SOME PEOPLE HAVE SUCH BAD FOOD ALLERGIES THAT EVEN *TOUCHING* SOMETHING WITH AN ALLERGEN CAN TRIGGER THE ALARM!

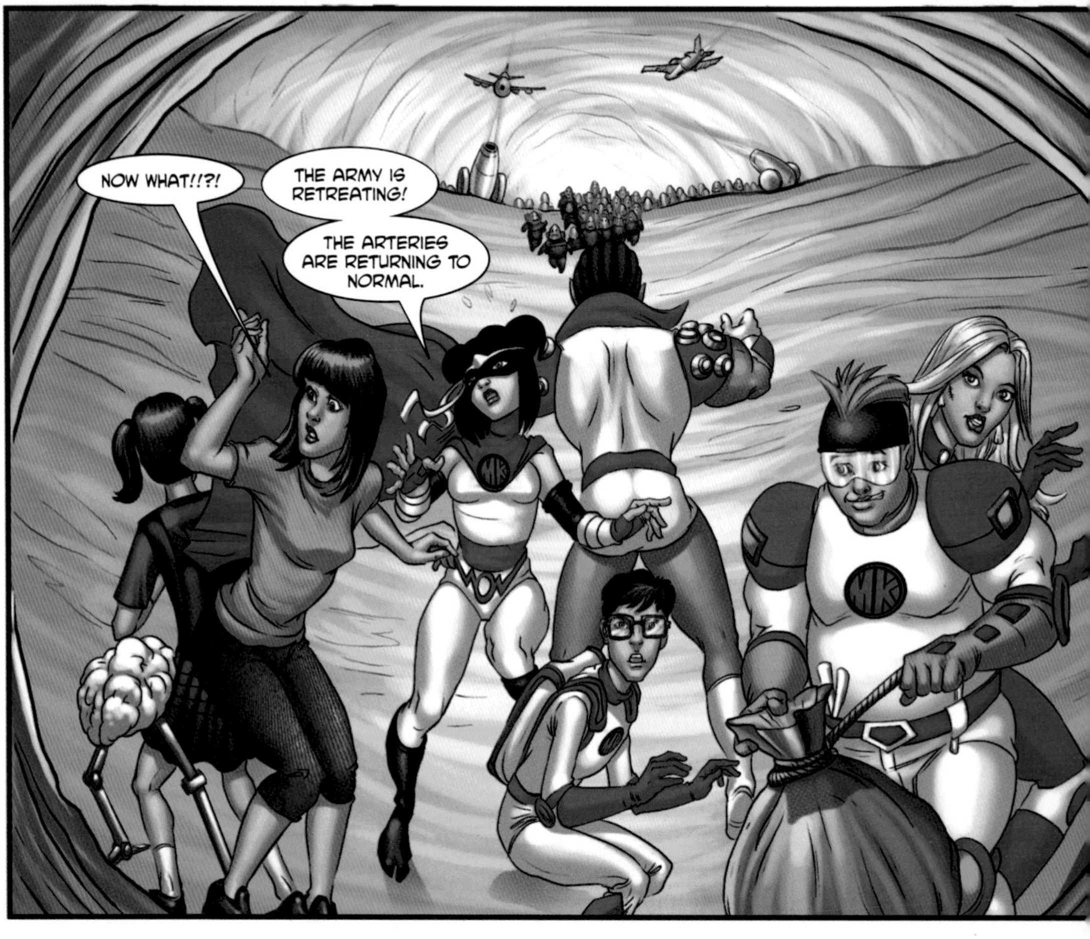
NOW WHAT!!?!
THE ARMY IS RETREATING!
THE ARTERIES ARE RETURNING TO NORMAL.

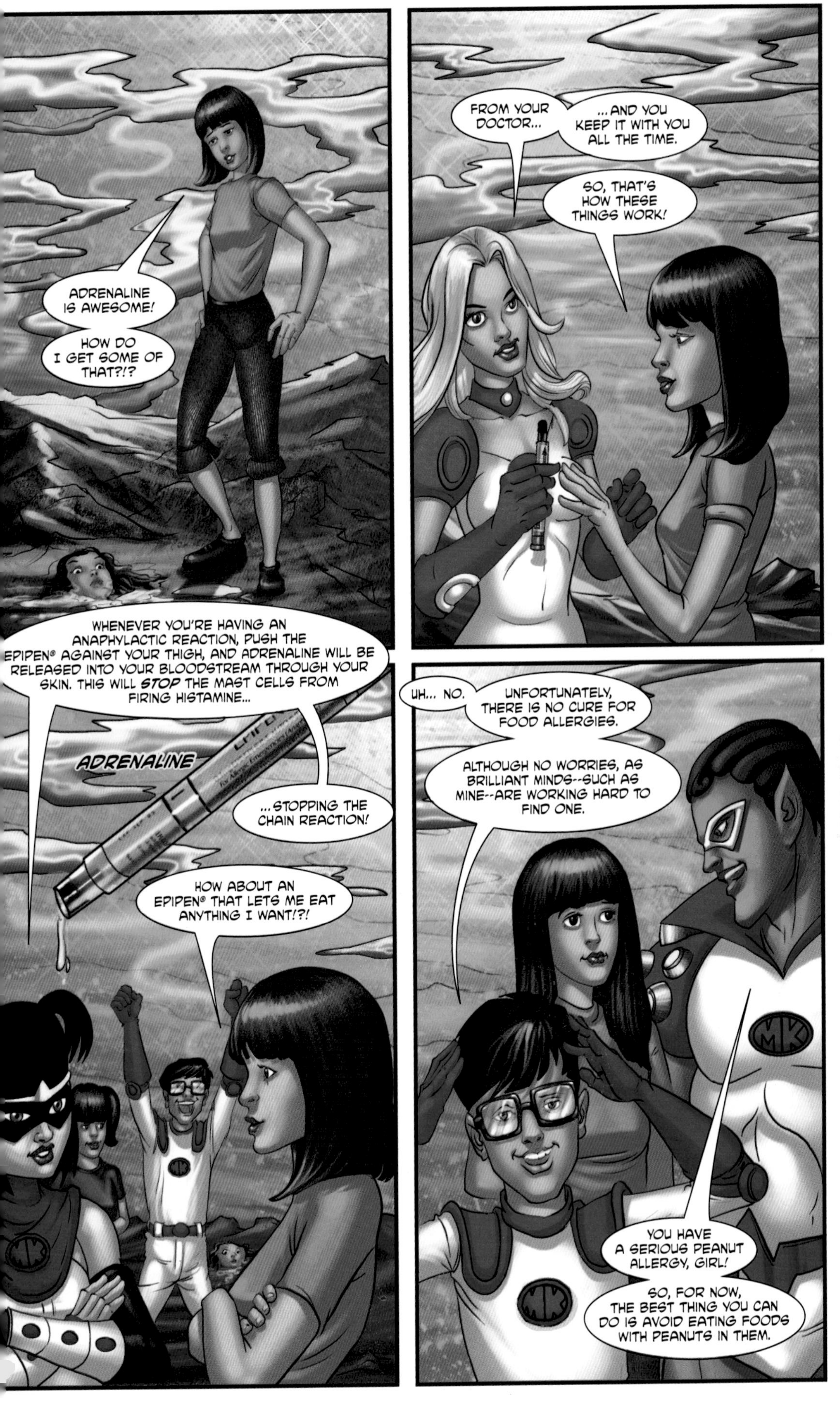
ADRENALINE IS AWESOME!
HOW DO I GET SOME OF THAT?!?
FROM YOUR DOCTOR...
...AND YOU KEEP IT WITH YOU ALL THE TIME.
SO, THAT'S HOW THESE THINGS WORK!
WHENEVER YOU'RE HAVING AN ANAPHYLACTIC REACTION, PUSH THE EPIPEN® AGAINST YOUR THIGH, AND ADRENALINE WILL BE RELEASED INTO YOUR BLOODSTREAM THROUGH YOUR SKIN. THIS WILL *STOP* THE MAST CELLS FROM FIRING HISTAMINE...
ADRENALINE
...STOPPING THE CHAIN REACTION!
HOW ABOUT AN EPIPEN® THAT LETS ME EAT ANYTHING I WANT!?!
UH... NO.
UNFORTUNATELY, THERE IS NO CURE FOR FOOD ALLERGIES.
ALTHOUGH NO WORRIES, AS BRILLIANT MINDS--SUCH AS MINE--ARE WORKING HARD TO FIND ONE.
YOU HAVE A SERIOUS PEANUT ALLERGY, GIRL!
SO, FOR NOW, THE BEST THING YOU CAN DO IS AVOID EATING FOODS WITH PEANUTS IN THEM.

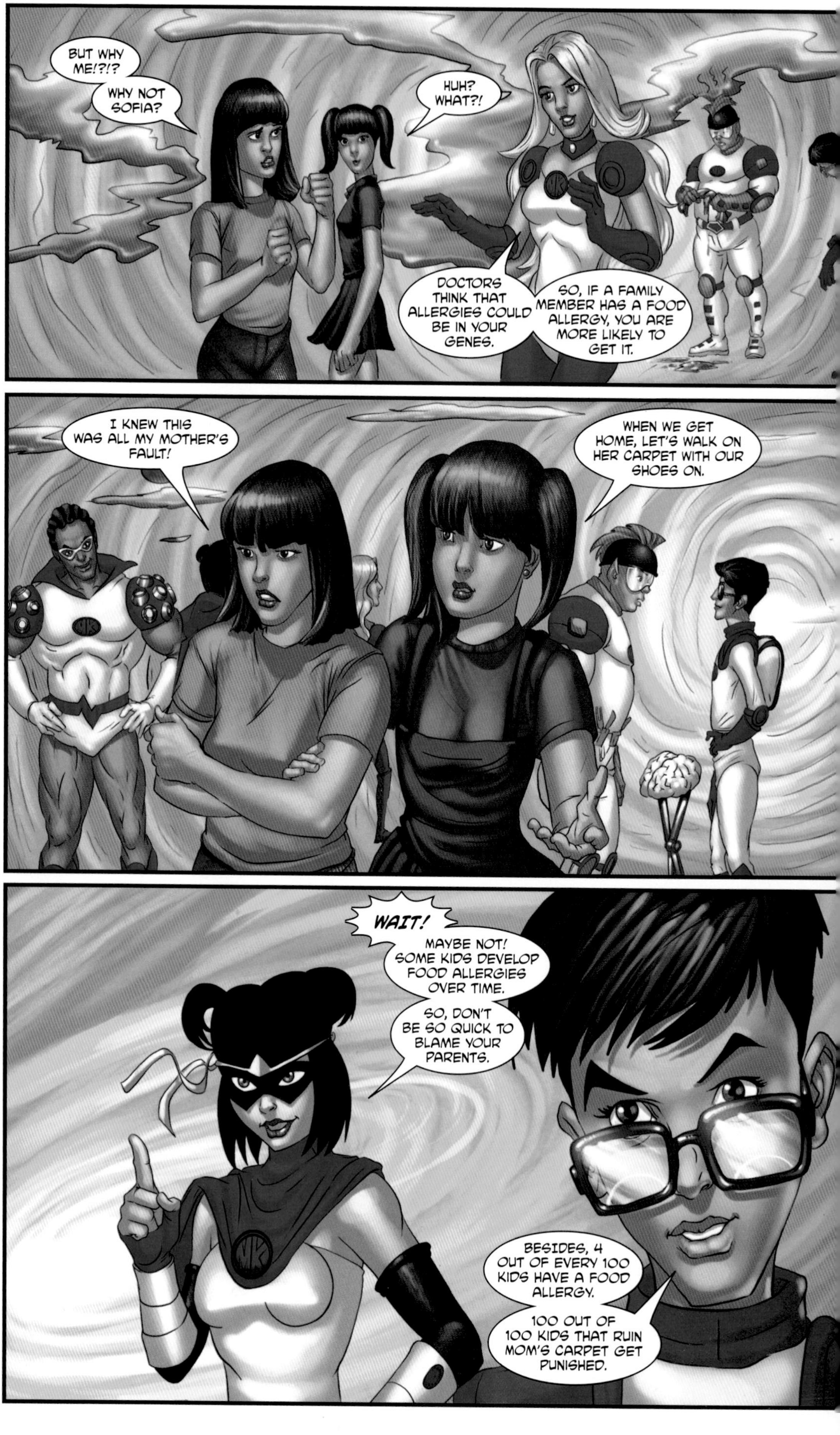
BUT WHY ME!?!?
WHY NOT SOFIA?
HUH? WHAT?!
DOCTORS THINK THAT ALLERGIES COULD BE IN YOUR GENES.
SO, IF A FAMILY MEMBER HAS A FOOD ALLERGY, YOU ARE MORE LIKELY TO GET IT.
I KNEW THIS WAS ALL MY MOTHER'S FAULT!
WHEN WE GET HOME, LET'S WALK ON HER CARPET WITH OUR SHOES ON.
WAIT!
MAYBE NOT! SOME KIDS DEVELOP FOOD ALLERGIES OVER TIME.
SO, DON'T BE SO QUICK TO BLAME YOUR PARENTS.
BESIDES, 4 OUT OF EVERY 100 KIDS HAVE A FOOD ALLERGY.
100 OUT OF 100 KIDS THAT RUIN MOM'S CARPET GET PUNISHED.

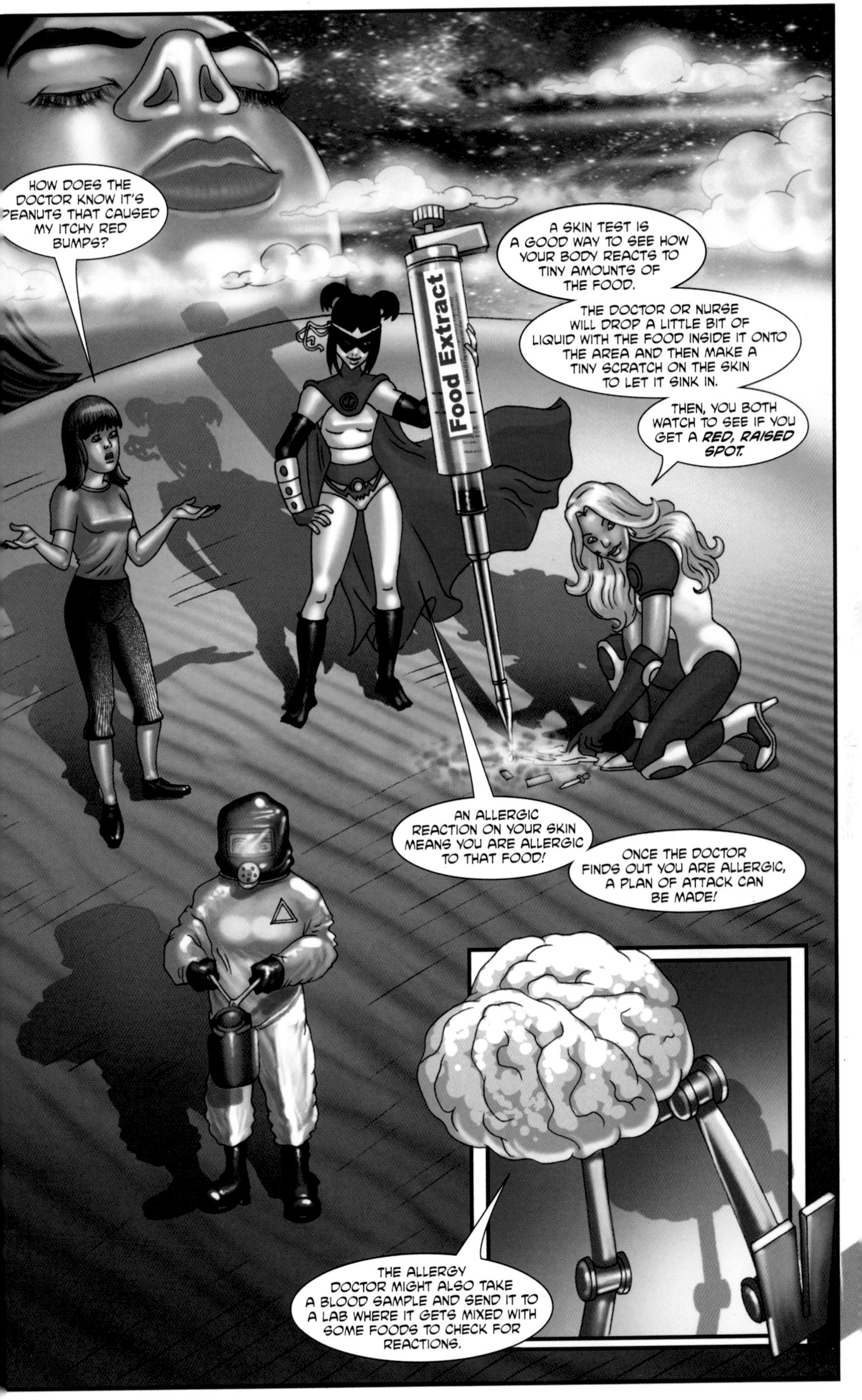
HOW DOES THE DOCTOR KNOW IT'S PEANUTS THAT CAUSED MY ITCHY RED BUMPS?
A SKIN TEST IS A GOOD WAY TO SEE HOW YOUR BODY REACTS TO TINY AMOUNTS OF THE FOOD.
THE DOCTOR OR NURSE WILL DROP A LITTLE BIT OF LIQUID WITH THE FOOD INSIDE IT ONTO THE AREA AND THEN MAKE A TINY SCRATCH ON THE SKIN TO LET IT SINK IN.
THEN, YOU BOTH WATCH TO SEE IF YOU GET A ***RED, RAISED SPOT.***
Food Extract
AN ALLERGIC REACTION ON YOUR SKIN MEANS YOU ARE ALLERGIC TO THAT FOOD!
ONCE THE DOCTOR FINDS OUT YOU ARE ALLERGIC, A PLAN OF ATTACK CAN BE MADE!
THE ALLERGY DOCTOR MIGHT ALSO TAKE A BLOOD SAMPLE AND SEND IT TO A LAB WHERE IT GETS MIXED WITH SOME FOODS TO CHECK FOR REACTIONS.

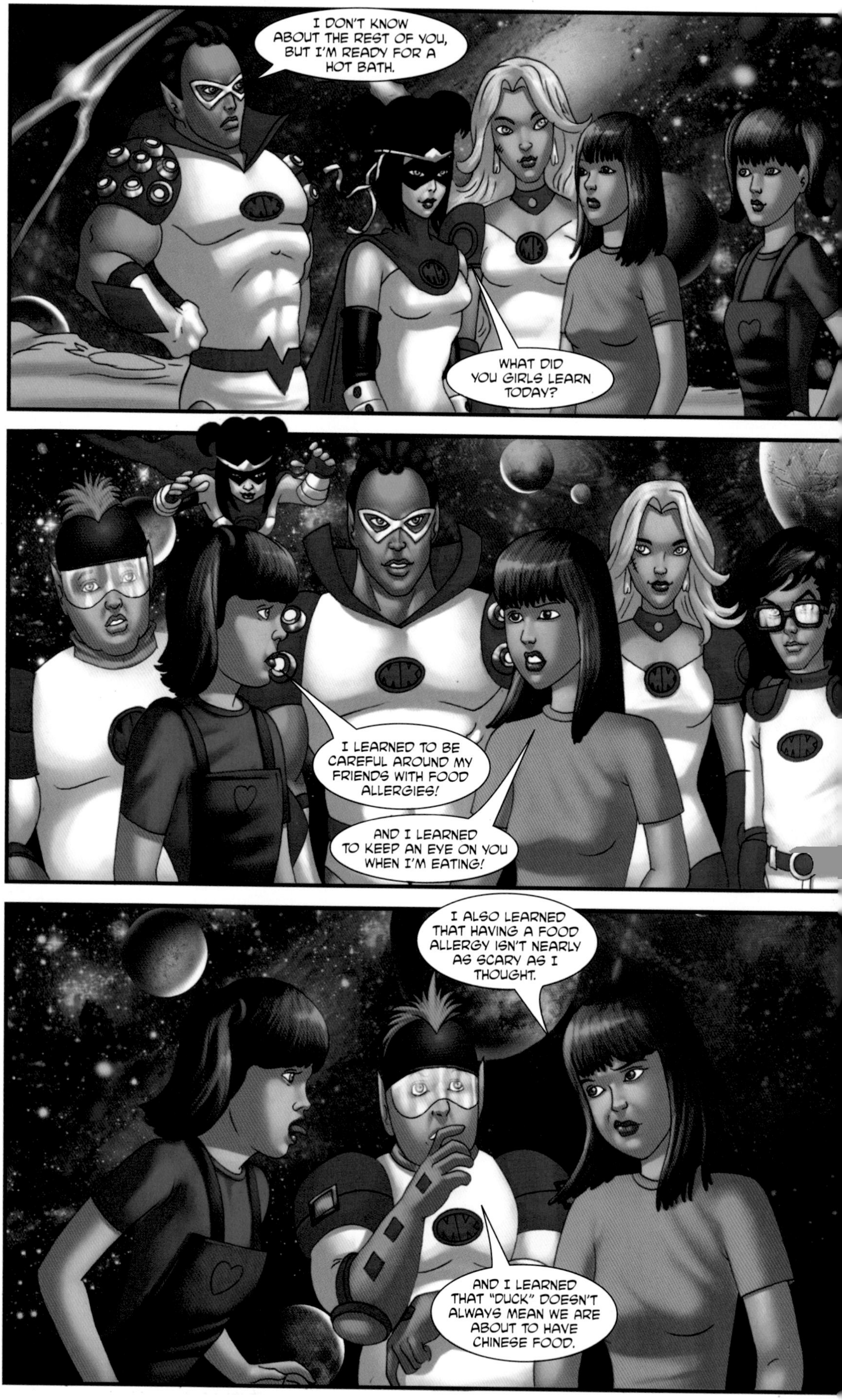
I DON'T KNOW ABOUT THE REST OF YOU, BUT I'M READY FOR A HOT BATH.
WHAT DID YOU GIRLS LEARN TODAY?
I LEARNED TO BE CAREFUL AROUND MY FRIENDS WITH FOOD ALLERGIES!
AND I LEARNED TO KEEP AN EYE ON YOU WHEN I'M EATING!
I ALSO LEARNED THAT HAVING A FOOD ALLERGY ISN'T NEARLY AS SCARY AS I THOUGHT.
AND I LEARNED THAT "DUCK" DOESN'T ALWAYS MEAN WE ARE ABOUT TO HAVE CHINESE FOOD.

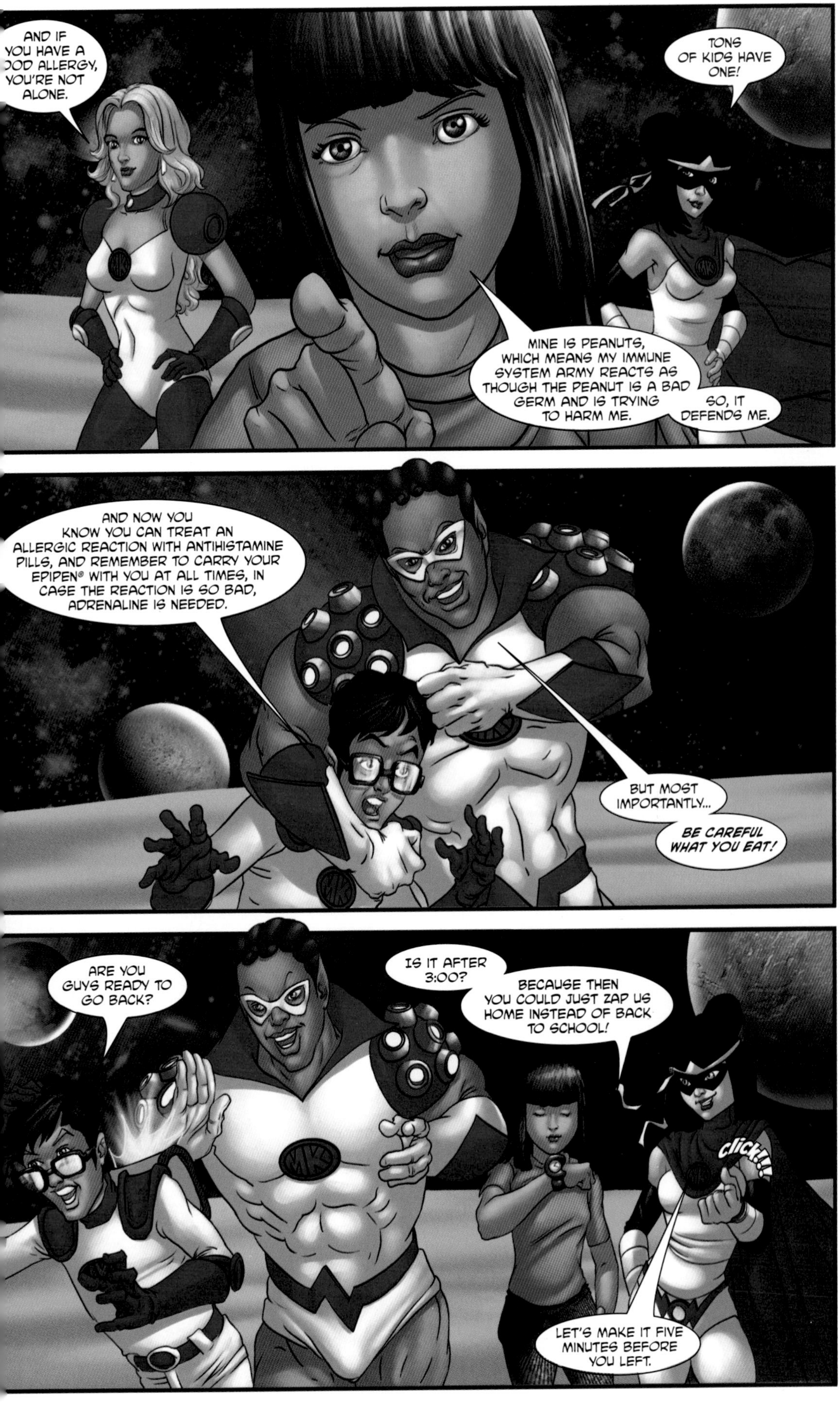
AND IF YOU HAVE A OOD ALLERGY, YOU'RE NOT ALONE.
TONS OF KIDS HAVE ONE!
MINE IS PEANUTS, WHICH MEANS MY IMMUNE SYSTEM ARMY REACTS AS THOUGH THE PEANUT IS A BAD GERM AND IS TRYING TO HARM ME.
SO, IT DEFENDS ME.
AND NOW YOU KNOW YOU CAN TREAT AN ALLERGIC REACTION WITH ANTIHISTAMINE PILLS, AND REMEMBER TO CARRY YOUR EPIPEN® WITH YOU AT ALL TIMES, IN CASE THE REACTION IS SO BAD, ADRENALINE IS NEEDED.
BUT MOST IMPORTANTLY...
BE CAREFUL WHAT YOU EAT!
ARE YOU GUYS READY TO GO BACK?
IS IT AFTER 3:00?
BECAUSE THEN YOU COULD JUST ZAP US HOME INSTEAD OF BACK TO SCHOOL!
CLICK!!!
LET'S MAKE IT FIVE MINUTES BEFORE YOU LEFT.

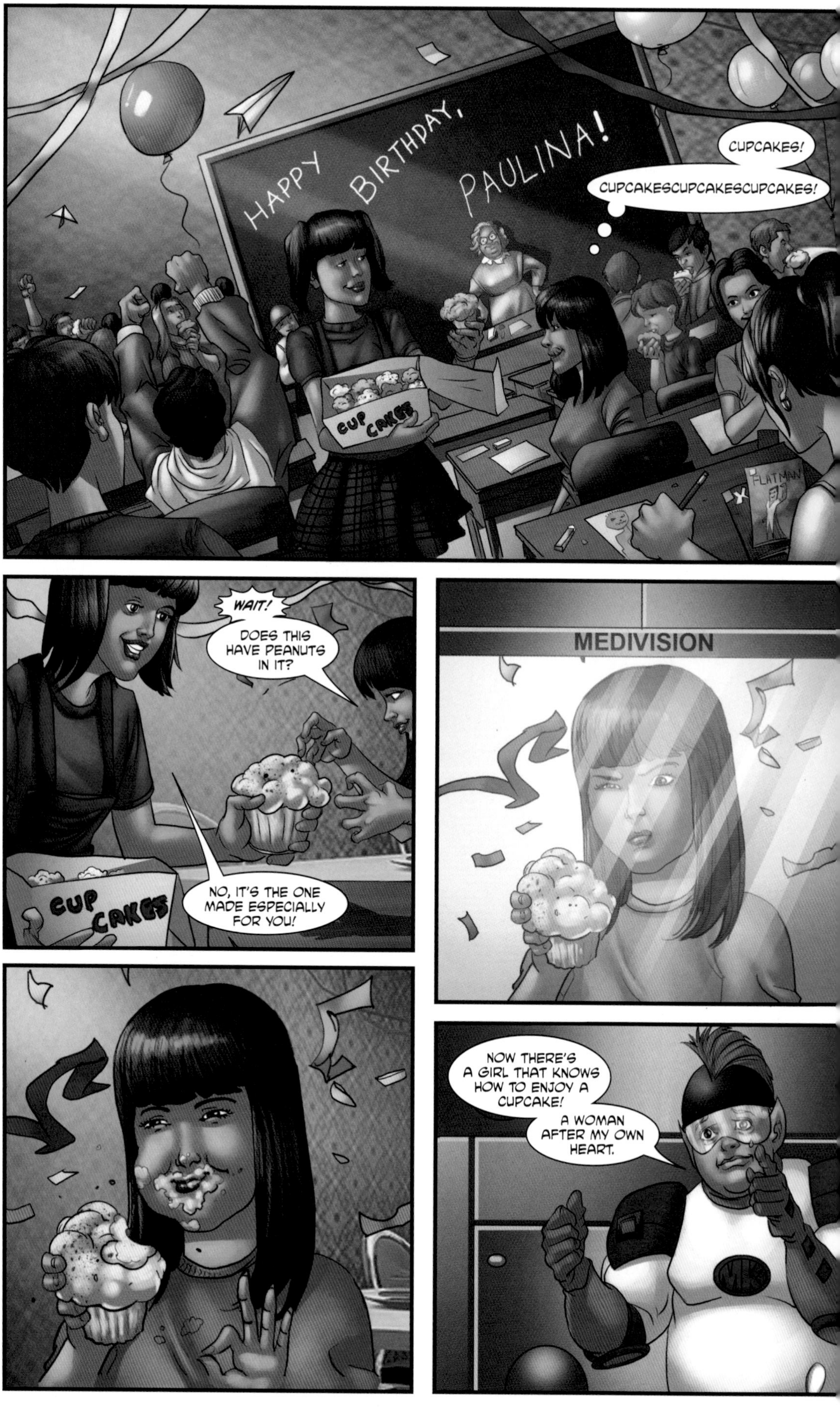
HAPPY BIRTHDAY, PAULINA!
CUPCAKES!
CUPCAKESCUPCAKESCUPCAKES!
CUP CAKES
FLATMAN
WAIT!
DOES THIS HAVE PEANUTS IN IT?
NO, IT'S THE ONE MADE ESPECIALLY FOR YOU!
CUP CAKES
MEDIVISION
NOW THERE'S A GIRL THAT KNOWS HOW TO ENJOY A CUPCAKE!
A WOMAN AFTER MY OWN HEART.

GLOSSARY

ADRENALINE ANOTHER TERM FOR THE HORMONE EPINEPHRINE.

ALLERGY A REACTION OF THE IMMUNE SYSTEM TO SOMETHING
THAT DOESN'T BOTHER MOST PEOPLE. THE BODY REACTS THE
WAY IT WOULD TO AN ANTIGEN.

ANAPHYLAXIS A POTENTIALLY LIFE-THREATENING ALLERGIC
REACTION INVOLVING THE WHOLE BODY CHARACTERIZED BY
TIGHTENING OF THE AIRWAYS, RAPID AND WEAK PULSE, SKIN
RASH, NAUSEA, AND VOMITING.

ANTIBODY A TYPE OF PROTEIN PRODUCED BY THE IMMUNE
SYSTEM WHEN IT DETECTS HARMFUL SUBSTANCES.

ANTIGEN ANY SUBSTANCE THAT CAUSES YOUR IMMUNE SYSTEM
TO PRODUCE ANTIBODIES. THIS CAN INCLUDE CHEMICALS, BAC-
TERIA, VIRUSES, OR POLLEN.

ANTIHISTAMINE A MEDICINE THAT IS USED TO COUNTERACT
HISTAMINE IN THE BODY, USED FOR TREATING ALLERGIC
REACTIONS.

ARTERY THE BLOOD VESSELS THAT CARRY BLOOD AWAY FROM
THE HEART.

B CELL A TYPE OF WHITE BLOOD CELL THAT MAKES
ANTIBODIES.

BACTERIA UNICELLULAR MICROORGANISMS. SOME ARE
CAPABLE OF CAUSING INFECTIOUS DISEASE, BUT MOST
ARE ACTUALLY A NECESSARY PART OF HUMAN LIFE.

BLOOD BODILY FLUID THAT DELIVERS NUTRIENTS AND OXYGEN
TO CELLS IN THE BODY AND ALSO TRANSPORTS WASTE
PRODUCTS AWAY FROM CELLS.

EPINEPHRINE HORMONE RELEASED INTO THE BLOODSTREAM
THAT SIGNALS THE HEART TO PUMP HARDER, INCREASES
BLOOD PRESSURE, AND OPENS AIRWAYS IN THE LUNGS.

EPIPEN® AN AUTO INJECTOR OF EPINEPHRINE USED TO TREAT
ANAPHYLACTIC SHOCK.

HEART THE MUSCULAR ORGAN OF THE CIRCULATORY SYSTEM
THAT IS RESPONSIBLE FOR PUMPING BLOOD THROUGHOUT
THE BODY.

HISTAMINE CHEMICAL RELEASED BY THE BODY DURING ALLER-
GIC REACTIONS THAT CAUSES DILATION OF CAPILLARIES,
CONTRACTION OF SMOOTH MUSCLE, AND STIMULATION OF
GASTRIC ACID SECRETION.

HIVES ALLERGIC REACTION CHARACTERIZED BY RAISED PATCHES
OF SKIN AND INTENSE ITCHING.

IMMUNE SYSTEM A GROUP OF SPECIAL CELLS, PROTEINS,
TISSUES, AND ORGANS THAT SEEK OUT AND DESTROY
ORGANISMS OR SUBSTANCES THAT CAUSE DISEASE.

MEDIC ALERT BRACELET A BRACELET THAT IS ENGRAVED WITH IDENTIFICATION AND MEDICAL CONDITION WORN BY SEVERE ALLERGY SUFFERERS IN ORDER TO BE MORE EASILY ASSISTED IN AN EMERGENCY.

PARASITE AN ORGANISM THAT LIVES IN, WITH, OR ON ANOTHER ORGANISM AND DEPENDS ON IT FOR SURVIVAL.

SKIN THE MULTILAYERED OUTER COVERING OF THE BODY THAT PROTECTS UNDERLYING TISSUES AND ORGANS AND REGULATES BODY HEAT, AMONG OTHER IMPORTANT FUNCTIONS.

STOMACH THE ORGAN IN THE DIGESTIVE SYSTEM WHERE THE BULK OF DIGESTION OCCURS.

VIRUS A MICROSCOPIC INFECTIOUS AGENT THAT CAN REPRODUCE ONLY INSIDE A HOST CELL.

WHITE BLOOD CELLS CELLS THAT DEFEND THE BODY AGAINST DISEASE AND FOREIGN MATERIALS.

FOR MORE INFORMATION

ALLERGY/ASTHMA INFORMATION ASSOCIATION
111 ZENWAY BOULEVARD, UNIT 1
VAUGHAN, ON L4H 3H9
CANADA
(800) 611-7011
WEB SITE: HTTP://AAIA.CA
THIS CHARITY ORGANIZATION IS DEDICATED TO HELPING ALLERGIC
INDIVIDUALS AND THEIR FAMILIES LEAD A NORMAL LIFE.

FOOD ALLERGY & ANAPHYLAXIS NETWORK
11781 LEE JACKSON HIGHWAY, SUITE 160
FAIRFAX, VA 22033
(800) 929-4040
WEB SITE: HTTP://WWW.FOODALLERGY.ORG
THIS ORGANIZATION IS DEDICATED TO RAISING PUBLIC AWARE-
NESS, PROVIDING ADVOCACY AND EDUCATION, AND ADVANCING
RESEARCH ON BEHALF OF ALL THOSE AFFECTED BY FOOD
ALLERGIES AND ANAPHYLAXIS.

FOOD ALLERGY INITIATIVE
1414 AVENUE OF THE AMERICAS, SUITE 1804
NEW YORK, NY 10019-2514
(212) 207-1974
WEB SITE: HTTP://WWW.FAIUSA.ORG
THIS ORGANIZATION WAS FOUNDED TO HELP FUND RESEARCH TO
SEEK A CURE, IMPROVE DIAGNOSIS AND TREATMENT, AND
KEEP PATIENTS SAFE THROUGH EDUCATION AND ADVOCACY.

KIDS WITH FOOD ALLERGIES, INC.
73 OLD DUBLIN PIKE, SUITE 10, #163
DOYLESTOWN, PA 18901
(215) 230-5394
WEB SITE: HTTP://WWW.KIDSWITHFOODALLERGIES.ORG
THIS NATIONAL NONPROFIT ORGANIZATION IS DEDICATED TO
FOSTERING OPTIMAL HEALTH, NUTRITION, AND WELL-BEING OF
CHILDREN WITH FOOD ALLERGIES BY PROVIDING EDUCATION
AND A CARING SUPPORT COMMUNITY FOR THEIR FAMILIES AND
CAREGIVERS.

MEDICALERT FOUNDATION INTERNATIONAL
2323 COLORADO AVENUE
TURLOCK, CA 95382
(888) 633-4298

WEB SITE: HTTP://WWW.MEDICALERT.ORG
THIS NONPROFIT HEALTHCARE INFORMATICS ORGANIZATION HELPS
    SAVE LIVES BY PROVIDING ACCESS TO THE RECORDS OF
    PEOPLE WITH POTENTIALLY LIFE-THREATENING CONDITIONS.

WORLD ALLERGY ORGANIZATION
555 EAST WELLS STREET, SUITE 1100
MILWAUKEE, WI 53202-3823
(414) 276-1791
WEB SITE: HTTP://WWW.WORLDALLERGY.ORG
THIS INTERNATIONAL ORGANIZATION UNITES ALLERGISTS AND
    IMMUNOLOGISTS FROM AROUND THE WORLD IN PROMOTING
    RESEARCH AND THE PRACTICE OF ALLERGY TREATMENT.

WEB SITES

DUE TO THE CHANGING NATURE OF INTERNET LINKS, ROSEN
PUBLISHING HAS DEVELOPED AN ONLINE LIST OF WEB SITES
RELATED TO THE SUBJECT OF THIS BOOK. THIS SITE IS UPDATED
REGULARLY. PLEASE USE THIS LINK TO ACCESS THE LIST:

HTTP://WWW.ROSENLINKS.COM/MED/ALLER

FOR FURTHER READING

BOCK, KENNETH, AND CAMERON STAUTH. *HEALING THE NEW CHILDHOOD EPIDEMICS: AUTISM, ADHD, ASTHMA, AND ALLERGIES: THE GROUNDBREAKING PROGRAM FOR THE 4-A DISORDERS.* NEW YORK, NY: RANDOM HOUSE, 2008.

DUMKE, NICOLETTE M. *ULTIMATE FOOD ALLERGY COOKBOOK AND SURVIVAL GUIDE: HOW TO COOK WITH EASE FOR A FOOD ALLERGY DIET AND RECOVER GOOD HEALTH.* AUSTIN, TX: ADAPT BOOKS, 2006.

FENSTER, CAROL. *COOKING FREE: 200 FLAVORFUL RECIPES FOR PEOPLE WITH FOOD ALLERGIES AND MULTIPLE FOOD SENSITIVITIES.* NEW YORK, NY: PENGUIN, 2005.

FREUND, LEE. *THE COMPLETE IDIOT'S GUIDE TO FOOD ALLERGIES.* NEW YORK, NY: PENGUIN, 2003.

HAMMOND, LESLIE, AND LYNNE MARIE ROMINGER. *KID-FRIENDLY FOOD ALLERGY COOKBOOK: MORE THAN 150 RECIPES THAT ARE: WHEAT-FREE, GLUTEN-FREE, DAIRY-FREE, NUT-FREE, EGG-FREE, LOW IN SUGAR.* BEVERLY, MA: FAIR WINDS PRESS, 2004.

KOELLER, KIM M., AND ROBERT R. LA FRANCE. *LET'S EAT OUT! YOUR PASSPORT TO LIVING GLUTEN AND ALLERGY FREE.* CHICAGO, IL: R & R PUBLISHING, 2005.

KORN, DANNA, AND ALESSIO FASANO. *LIVING GLUTEN-FREE FOR DUMMIES.* HOBOKEN, NJ: WILEY, 2006.

KRAYNAK, JOE, AND ROBERT A. WOOD, M.D. *FOOD ALLERGIES FOR DUMMIES.* HOBOKEN, NJ: WILEY, 2007.

LOWELL, JAX PETERS, AND ANTHONY J. DIMARINO. *GLUTEN-FREE BIBLE: THE THOROUGHLY INDISPENSABLE GUIDE TO NEGOTIATING LIFE WITHOUT WHEAT.* NEW YORK, NY: HENRY HOLT, 2005.

LUCAS, GLENIS. *COMPLETE GUIDE TO GLUTEN-FREE AND DAIRY-FREE COOKING: OVER 200 DELICIOUS RECIPES.* LONDON, UK: DUNCAN BAIRD, 2006.

OH, CHAD, AND CAROL KENNEDY. *HOW TO LIVE WITH A NUT ALLERGY.* NEW YORK, NY: MCGRAW-HILL, 2004.

RICHER, ALICE C. *FOOD ALLERGIES.* SANTA BARBARA, CA: GREENWOOD PUBLISHING, 2009.

SICHERER, SCOTT H. *UNDERSTANDING AND MANAGING YOUR CHILD'S FOOD ALLERGIES.* BALTIMORE, MD: JOHNS HOPKINS, 2006.

SICHERER, SCOTT H., AND TERRY MALLOY. *THE COMPLETE PEANUT ALLERGY HANDBOOK.* NEW YORK, NY: PENGUIN, 2005.

YODER, ELLEN RHUDE. *THE ALLERGY-FREE COOKBOOK: MORE THAN 150 DELICIOUS RECIPES FOR A HAPPY AND HEALTHY DIET.* PHILADELPHIA, PA: RUNNING PRESS, 2009.

INDEX

ABOUT THE AUTHORS

DR. KIM CHILMAN-BLAIR IS A MEDICAL DOCTOR WITH TEN YEARS' EXPERIENCE OF MEDICAL WRITING, AND A PASSION FOR PROVIDING MEDICAL INFORMATION THAT MAKES CHILDREN WANT TO LEARN.

JOHN TADDEO, FORMALLY OF MARVEL ENTERTAINMENT, IS A CELEBRATED COMIC BOOK WRITER AND DIRECTOR OF TWO AWARD-WINNING ANIMATED SHORTS.